ML
429
J43
C7

Cripe, Helen.
Thomas Jefferson and music. Charlottesville, University Press of Virginia [1974]

viii, 157 p. illus., facsims. 25 cm.

"Jefferson's catalogue of 1783; transcription of the music section": p. [97]–104.
"Collections of Jefferson family music": p. [105]–128.
Bibliography: p. [135]–152.

1. Jefferson, Thomas, Pres. U. S., 1743–1826—Music. I. Title.

ML429.J43C7 780'.92'4 167 73–81099
ISBN 0–8139–0504–4 MARC

Library of Congress 74 [4] MN

Thomas Jefferson and Music

Thomas Jefferson and Music

Helen Cripe

University Press of Virginia
Charlottesville

THE UNIVERSITY PRESS OF VIRGINIA

First published 1974

ISBN: 0–8139–0504–4
Library of Congress Catalog Card Number: 73–81099
Printed in the United States of America

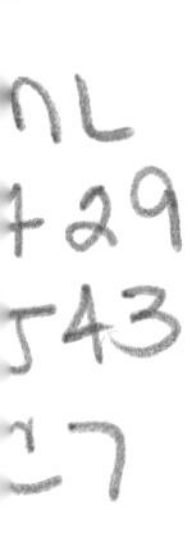

To the memory of

Herbert Richard Cripe, Jr.

February 18, 1933–January 21, 1970

"a kind and generous life"

Acknowledgments

I WISH to thank the following institutions for the assistance they have given me during the writing of this book: University of Notre Dame Library; Manuscripts Reading Room and Rare Book Room, University of Virginia Library; Manuscripts Reading Room, Music Division, Periodicals Division and Rare Book Room, Library of Congress; Manuscripts Division, University of North Carolina Library; Massachusetts Historical Society; Musical Instruments Room, Boston Museum of Fine Arts; Colonial Williamsburg Research Library; Musical Instruments Division, Smithsonian Institution; Henry E. Huntington Library and Art Gallery; University of Notre Dame History Department; University of Notre Dame Music Department; University of Virginia Music Department; Curator's Office, Monticello; Colonnade Club, University of Virginia.

I also wish to express my appreciation to the following individuals for substantial assistance as well as for insights arrived at in conversation during the progress of this work: James A. Bear, Jr., curator of Monticello, his assistant, Mrs. Susan Klaffky, and his researcher, Mrs. Lucia Goodwin; Mrs. Mary Goodwin, Colonial Williamsburg; Mrs. Helen Hollis, Musical Instruments Division, Smithsonian Institution; the members of Professor Marshall Smelser's predoctoral seminar, University of Notre Dame, 1968–69; Professor Eugene Leahy, Music Department, University of Notre Dame; E. O. Witt, harpsichord builder, Three Rivers, Michigan; David Tetrault, harpsichordist, University of Virginia; Mrs. Carolyn Galbraith Nolan, Roanoke, Virginia; Dumas Malone, Merrill Peterson, Robert Rutland, and Donald Jackson, all of the University of Virginia; Harold J. Coolidge; Walter Muir Whitehill; Helen D. Bullock; Mrs. James Watts, "Poplar Forest"; the Reverend Thomas E. Blantz, C.S.C., and Professor M. A. Fitzsimons, my two "bosses" at Notre Dame; Mr. and Mrs. James Silver; Miss Donna Purvis and Ms. Patricia Mahoney, my typists.

I am indebted to *Antiques* magazine (July 1972) for material contained in my article "Music: Thomas Jefferson's 'Delightful Recreation,' " as well as for the cover illustration, the frontispiece, and other pictures.

I extend very special thanks to Professor Marshall Smelser, Department of History, University of Notre Dame, for guiding me through two years of good times, bad times, and unique experiences. I also thank his wife, Anna, who volunteered for an equally maddening job—that of attempting to teach this historian to play Mr. Jefferson's instrument, the violin.

Finally, there would have been no study without the encouragement and help of my late husband, Herbert Cripe, Jr.

University of Notre Dame
April 4, 1972

Contents

Illustrations

Figures in Text

Thomas Jefferson and Music

Abbreviations

TJ Thomas Jefferson

Depositories

CSmH Henry E. Huntington Library and Art Gallery, San Marino, California
DLC Library of Congress
MHi Massachusetts Historical Society, Boston
NcU University of North Carolina Library
ViU University of Virginia Library

Manuscript Collections

EHR Edgehill Randolph Papers
EWC Ellen Wayles Coolidge Correspondence
NPT Nicholas Philip Trist Papers
SRM Septimia Randolph Meikleham Papers

Multivolume Works

Account Books: Thomas Jefferson's Account Books, 1767–1826, typescript by James A. Bear, Jr.
The multivolume works of Dumas Malone, Julian Boyd, and Henry S. Randall are cited by the last name of the author or editor and a Roman numeral designating the volume used, e.g., Malone I, or Boyd IX. *Grove's Dictionary of Music and Musicians* is cited, Grove, with the appropriate volume number, e.g., Grove V.

Introduction

THE OLD HARPSICHORD remained in the house several years after the family went away. Curiosity-seekers occasionally mentioned it, usually commenting on its wretched condition—the rattling plunk of its keys and the mournful sound of its long-untuned voice. It must have been in terrible shape, otherwise one of the grandchildren would surely have kept it or sold it along with the house and furnishings. But battered beyond repair as it was, there was nothing sad about this particular old harpsichord; it got that way because the people who loved it played it constantly for nearly forty years.

The harpsichord's long and useful life began in a London shop in 1786, where it was built according to the exact specifications of a better-than-average amateur musician who wanted a superb instrument for his talented elder daughter. The gentleman himself was in Paris at the time and could not personally oversee its construction, so he asked several of his friends to look after its building and "playing-in," and to ship it to him when the maker completed it. After many months, it crossed the Channel to a temporary home with its delighted young mistress in Paris. Two years later it crossed the Atlantic, ending its travels by riding in a straw-filled wagon to the house atop a small mountain near Charlottesville, Virginia. And there it stood for the rest of its life, watching a veritable procession of other keyboard instruments pass into and out of Monticello, still beloved by its mistress even when it reached the stage where one of her daughters called it "Mama's old rattle-trap." And there it still stood in 1830, somewhat unsteadily to be sure, after the family had left Monticello forever.

It is surprising that so much of the Jefferson family music has survived; in the University of Virginia Library there are seven file boxes of it, plus several recent acquisitions, all deposited in a safe place at last after having passed through the hands of several generations of the family. The collection reflects the tastes of a man who, by means of copious purchase and constant exchange with friends, accumulated a potpourri of every kind of music available and in every possible arrangement that he, his family, and friends could play or sing. Some of this music survived because Jefferson had many of the individual selections beautifully bound into large thick volumes. Scattered through the music is ample evidence that Jefferson and his family loved every bit of it and used it constantly. One can easily identify Jefferson's distinctive writing as well as his daughter Martha Randolph's delicately precise script among the hands of many unknown annotators. Someone wrote in notations for fingering for many of the keyboard selections. Small grandchildren and their host of cousins and friends added childish doodles and scribbles. Mrs. Jefferson, Martha, and several granddaughters made many beautiful manuscript copies of family favorites. Jefferson himself made lists of music he hoped to acquire, wrote directions for tuning harpsichords, and copied the words of his favorite psalms into the printed music. The remnants of the music collection, an old square piano, a guitar, a music rack, and two music stands remain as the only tangible evidence of the musical interests of this versatile man.

"Music," wrote Jefferson at seventy-four, "is invaluable where a person has an ear. It furnishes a delightful recreation for the hours of respite from the cares of the day, and lasts us through life."[1] Jefferson's delightful recreation certainly did last him through life, and he devoted a surprising amount of time to it, considering the scope of his better-known activities. Neither the exigencies of his public career, the ever-precarious state of his finances, nor the later physical discomforts of an injured wrist ever caused him to desert his music completely, although in his last years he became more of a listener than a participant.

He liked all kinds of music, from baroque violin sonatas to sentimental ballads. His first love was the violin. He was not just another country fiddler, but was a violinist of more than average skill, who had learned to read music and who played the best current violin literature from Europe as well as Virginia hill tunes. There is no evidence that any of Jefferson's violins still exist; in fact, it is impossible to determine exactly how many violins he had, their make, and their present whereabouts. They, like his keyboard instruments, came and went.

Granddaughters and friends frequently mentioned his clear singing voice and his enjoyment of singing in the home. He could not play keyboard instruments, although several times in later life he said he wished he had learned to play them. He carefully supervised

[1] TJ to Nathaniel Burwell, Esq., Mar. 14, 1818, Andrew A. Lipscomb and Albert Ellery Bergh, eds., *The Writings of Thomas Jefferson* (Washington, 1903–4), XV, 135.

the musical education of his daughters and granddaughters, insisting upon the finest instruction available and on high standards of performance. His extensive collection of music included volumes of instruction and technique as well as contemporary vocal and instrumental selections chosen for sheer pleasure. He was a discriminating purchaser of superior musical instruments, and he made himself an authority on their construction and maintenance. His correspondence reveals a skillful technician's fascination with how musical instruments worked and what innovations could improve them. Jefferson obviously did enjoy the functional; however, only an equally strong aesthetic appreciation could account for the variety of his music collection, his enjoyment of playing and of listening to others play, and his constant admonitions to his daughters to keep up with their music despite household chores, small children, illnesses, hordes of visitors, and all the other studies that he scheduled for them. "Do not neglect your music," he wrote to Martha Randolph in 1790. "It will be a companion which will sweeten many hours of life to you."[2]

Jefferson, in his own voluminous correspondence, did not really say much about music at all. He only discussed it with a few close friends and family members, and even to them he never philosophized about the position of music among the arts. He always expressed interest in what music his daughters were playing and he occasionally went into lavish detail in describing some form of musical gadgetry. It is easy to dismiss him as a musical mechanic after reading his correspondence with Francis Hopkinson concerning the quilling of harpsichords and the addition of a keyboard to the glass harmonica. One wonders if his taste in instruments did not verge on the capricious after noting all the special accessories he wanted built into Martha's harpsichord and upon discovering that he wanted a six-octave glass harmonica. But then there is always the evidence of his music collection. Surely no mere musical mechanic could have appreciated Vivaldi, Corelli, Boccherini, Haydn, and Mozart.

Jefferson as musician and music lover appears more clearly in the observations of family, friends, and acquaintances. The correspondence of two of his granddaughters, Ellen Randolph Coolidge and Virginia Randolph Trist, best describes his musical activities. Although these two ladies idolized their grandfather, their letters are intelligent, perceptive, and astringent, and their observations and opinions are totally believable. Both of the girls inherited the family musical talent and grew up at Monticello under the supervision of

[2] TJ to Martha Jefferson Randolph, April 4, 1790, Edwin Morris Betts and James A. Bear, Jr., eds., *The Family Letters of Thomas Jefferson* (Columbia, Mo., 1966), p. 51.

"dear Grandpapa." In addition, individuals among the crowds of relatives and visitors who flocked to Monticello recorded many intimate glimpses of the musical life of the Jefferson household.

Thus, with the aid of these fragments, it is possible to reveal another facet of the personality of a fascinating man and to show how much his delightful recreation meant to him.

CHAPTER I

American Secular Music of Jefferson's Time

THOMAS JEFFERSON once called American music barbarous.[1] In making this statement he was most unfair; for, although American music of his time may not have been uniformly excellent, a considerable amount of cultivated music taught and performed by capable and talented people was available in most areas for those who were interested in it. We cannot call much of it truly American music because practically all of it was imported from England. Moreover, nearly all professional musicians were immigrants—Germans, Englishmen, Italians, and Frenchmen. The important fact is that Americans, economically stable and by the latter eighteenth century politically independent, could afford to support a surprisingly large and varied musical culture.

Did all these immigrant professional musicians come to America because they were third-rate talents who could not compete in Europe? Probably not. Like professionals in any line of work, they went where they could find suitable recompense for their services, and Americans of that period were paying musicians well. More and more Americans were interested in purchasing good musical instruments. Printed music was in great demand, as were all other musical supplies such as music paper, music ruling pens, tuning hammers, and strings. Singing schools and émigré organists improved church music. Ballad opera, popular in England, was introduced into America. Public concerts and dancing assemblies sprang up everywhere. On the whole secular music developed much more rapidly than sacred music and became much more important. There was seldom a time in Jefferson's life, except perhaps after he retired to Monticello in 1809, that he could not have gone to hear, or to participate in, some performance of music. There was never a time when he could not have bought excellent musical instruments and stacks of music to play on them. And his accounts show that he never had trouble finding music and dancing teachers for his daughters.[2]

[1] TJ, Williamsburg, to Giovanni Fabbroni, June 8, 1778, Boyd II, 196.

[2] Maurer Maurer, "The Musical Life of Colonial America in the Eighteenth Century" (Ph.D. dissertation, Ohio State University, 1950), p. 362; Virginia Larkin Redway, "The Carrs, American Music Publishers," *Musical Quarterly*

How well did America support these immigrant professional musicians? Then, as now, sometimes very well and sometimes not at all. Above all, the professional musician had to be versatile. In addition to teaching either instrumental or vocal music, he might also teach dancing and, quite frequently, fencing. In rural areas such as Jefferson's Virginia, he rode a circuit, or perhaps families like the Jeffersons and the Carters commissioned him to stay with them for a specific length of time. In the larger cities he could establish himself more permanently: he played in concert and theater orchestras; he was usually a church organist; and he probably composed. Sometimes he tried his luck at music printing and publishing. Quite often he was, or had been, an actor. If he could not make his entire living from music, he augmented his income in many ways, and there are records of "professors of musick" who barbered, did accounting, drew up legal papers, took orders for chimney sweeping, and kept various kinds of shops.[3]

Peter Pelham, resident of Williamsburg for more than fifty years and well-known to Jefferson, is probably Virginia's best-known professional musician of the late eighteenth century. His father came from England when Peter was about five years old. After long and thorough training from Charles Theodore Pachelbel, another immigrant, young Pelham taught in several towns, was organist at Trinity Church in Boston for a few years, and came to Williamsburg about 1750. He assisted in the installation of the organ at Bruton Parish Church and was chosen organist. As was usual with musicians, he did a little of everything: he took pupils in organ and harpsichord; he tuned, built, and repaired instruments; he conducted performances of theater companies and church choirs and accompanied soloists; he composed, arranged, rehearsed, and performed music for all public occasions on which music was used; he organized concerts and usually performed in them. Despite all this activity, however, Pelham could not earn his entire livelihood from music. Various friends and patrons secured several civil posts for him. He was one of the commissioners supervising the printing of treasury notes. As clerk for governors Fauquier and Botetourt he took applications for tobacco inspections and issued ships' passes. During the Revolution he was keeper of the Public Gaol, for which he received forty pounds per

18 (1932): 150; Oscar G. Sonneck, *Early Concert Life in America (1731–1800)* (Leipzig, 1907), p. 9; John W. Molnar, "Art Music in Colonial Virginia," in *Art and Music in the South*, ed. by Francis B. Simkins (Farmville, Va., 1961), p. 63.

[3] Maurer Maurer, "The 'Professor of Musick' in Colonial America," *Musical Quarterly* 36 (1950): 511–24.

year and the privilege of living quarters on the premises. Pelham was on excellent terms, both socially and professionally, with the best Williamsburg society.[4]

Eighteenth-century America drew several interesting musical distinctions. Gentleman amateurs, such as Jefferson and Francis Hopkinson, were very definitely gentlemen, no matter how good they were as musicians, and as gentlemen they could never appear in any situation that might imply that they were receiving pay for their services. They did frequently play in public, usually in concerts or theater orchestras, but only as patrons, helping out their professor. The professor himself, even someone like Pelham, was socially on about the same level as a storekeeper or skilled craftsman. The professional musician let it be known that he did not furnish music for dances and other entertainments. That job belonged to servants. Many black slaves and white indentured servants could play instruments quite well. Evidence of their value as musicians appears in many advertisements in the *Virginia Gazette*. Persons seeking to acquire slaves or indentured servants often specified that in addition to the usual qualifications they wanted performers on certain instruments. Many advertisements for runaways mentioned as identification that the culprit could play some instrument.[5] Although it was fairly common for slaves to play instruments for dances, nobody paid much attention to Negro music as such, and songs about Negroes or in Negro dialect were very rare.[6]

Concerts and theatrical performances available to Jefferson and his contemporaries were plentiful, varied, and occasionally horrendous. Concerts were held in taverns, assembly rooms, gardens, halls, theaters, or churches. Often they were subscription concerts; patrons, by subscribing a certain amount of money, received tickets to a single concert or a series. When the musician organizing the concert had sufficient subscriptions, he proceeded to have it given. Concerts were often organized as benefits for unfortunates or for the musician himself; Peter Pelham's daughter and son-in-law gave a benefit concert for him in Williamsburg in 1777. Theatrical presenta-

[4] Maurer Maurer, "Peter Pelham: Organist-Jailer," *Tyler's Quarterly Historical and Genealogical Magazine* 28 (1946); Maurer, " 'Professor of Musick,' " p. 523; Richard Beale Davis, *Intellectual Life in Jefferson's Virginia, 1790–1830* (Chapel Hill, 1964), p. 231; Molnar, pp. 76–78.

[5] Maurer, " 'Professor of Musick,' " pp. 517, 523; Molnar, p. 69; Maurer, "Musical Life," pp. 150–51, 155–56; Albert L. Stoutamire, "A History of Music in Richmond, Virginia, from 1742 to 1865" (Ph.D. dissertation, Florida State University, 1960), pp. 13–14.

[6] Cyclone Covey, "Of Music and of America Singing," in Max Savelle, *Seeds of Liberty* (New York, 1948), p. 534.

tion followed the English closely in organization, performance, and repertory. Theatrical groups presented mostly ballad and comic operas and other forms of drama with or without music. Gentlemen amateur musicians filled out the orchestras and ensembles for both concerts and theatrical performances. The conductor (often Pelham, in Williamsburg) did not only conduct—he played the harpsichord as well, conducting while playing. Newspaper or other printed advertising for performances was scanty before the 1790s; the performance itself was announced, but those attending did not always know what they were going to hear. Titles of plays and operas, however, were usually announced in advance.[7]

Jefferson and his friends required endurance and frequent breaks for punch in order to survive some of these performances. The audience really got its money's worth. Both concerts and plays had dances and solo instrumental or vocal entr'actes. Sometimes the program would include two complete short plays. Afterwards there might be a ball, "if agreeable to the company," and it usually was. The *Virginia Gazette* announced a typical theatrical performance for April 15, 1768: a tragedy—*The Orphan*, or *The Unhappy Marriage*—to be followed by a "comick dance," *The Bedlamites*. On the second night there was to be added to these two a pantomime called *Harlequin Skeleton*, or *The Burgomaster Tricked*. The doors would open at 6:00 P.M. and the performance would begin at 7:00. Tickets for box seats cost 7s6d, pit 5s, and gallery 3s9d.[8]

Elaborate spectacles, complete with appropriate music, were also common. Jefferson was probably one of "the curious" who saw the following performance at Williamsburg in 1769:

> By Permission of his excellency the governor, for the entertainment of the curious: On Friday the 14th of this Instant April will be exhibited, at the theater in Williamsburg, by Peter Gardiner, a curious set of figures, richly dressed, four feet high, which shall appear upon the stage as if alive; to which will be added a tragedy called the Babes in the Wood; also a curious view of waterworks, representing the sea, with all manner of sea monsters sporting upon the waves. Likewise fireworks, together with the taking of the *Havannah*, with ships, forts, and batteries, continually firing, until victory crowns the conquest; to which will be added a curious field of battle, containing the Dutch, French, Prussian, and English forces, which shall regularly march and perform the different exercises to great perfection. The performer will lay his head on one chair and his feet on another, and suffer a large rock of 300 weight to be broke on his breast with a sledge hammer. Tickets to be had at the Raleigh

[7] Molnar, p. 76; Maurer, "Musical Life," pp. 352–53; Sonneck, p. 12.

[8] *Virginia Gazette*, Apr. 14, 1768.

Tavern. Box 3s9d. Pit 2s6d. Gallery 1s3d. The doors to be opened at four o'clock, and the entertainment to begin at six. None can be admitted without tickets, nor any admitted behind the scenes, as the inconvenience must be obvious. NB—None of the above is represented by way of an optic box, or peeping through glasses, but shall appear public on the stage, conspicuously to the view of the spectators, without confusion.[9]

Virginia audiences apparently did not always behave very well, possibly because of the various forms of punch that were so readily available. Several advertisements stress that no persons are to be admitted behind the scenes at the playhouses. For one particular concert the ladies requested "that the Company may be governed by a becoming silence and decorum, during the performance."[10]

Eighteenth-century Americans had a wide choice of music, almost all of it from London. It was not necessarily great music, but Americans enjoyed listening to it and playing it. Much of it required a high degree of training and proficiency, and many amateurs could perform it creditably. Jefferson's own collection of music (examined in detail in Chapter VI and Appendix II) was remarkable in quality, quantity, and scope; in fact he had some of practically every kind of music heard anywhere in America. Cuthbert Ogle, who died before he could make a beginning as a music teacher in Williamsburg, left an estate consisting of a large bundle of English, German, and Italian music, along with a violin and a harpsichord. Robert Carter of Nomini Hall and many other wealthy planters probably had music libraries as large and varied as Jefferson's, if not more so.[11]

By the middle of the eighteenth century, American merchants were selling almost any music then available in England, and by the end of the century several Americans were printing and publishing music. The most prominent of these early American music publishers was the Carr family, of Philadelphia, New York, and Baltimore.[12] Although original American music was both scanty and generally pretty bad, Philadelphians such as Alexander Reinagle, John Christopher Moller, and the Von Hagens were turning out some very respectable work during the 1790s. Cities such as Philadelphia and New York made it possible for music dealers to support themselves; in towns such as Williamsburg music could be purchased at the Printing Office, from a private individual who happened to have

[9] *Virginia Gazette*, Apr. 13, 1769.

[10] *Virginia Gazette*, May 11, 1769.

[11] Maurer Maurer, "The Library of a Colonial Musician, 1755," *William and Mary Quarterly* 7 (1950): 39–52; Lyon G. Tyler, ed., "Libraries in Colonial Virginia," Part II, *William and Mary Quarterly* 3 (1894–95): 251–53.

[12] Redway, "The Carrs, American Music Publishers."

some for sale, or from a shopkeeper who got a bundle of music along with his usual shipment of dry goods, clothing, jewelry, drugs, or confections.

American interest in music extended beyond instruction and performance. Americans bought and read a great number of books on music theory, history, and aesthetics. Jefferson owned several such volumes (see Chapter VI). Dr. Charles Burney, the most renowned eighteenth-century English authority on music, was well known to Jefferson, Robert Carter, and others through his *History of Music*, *Present State of Music in Germany*, and *Present State of Music in Italy*. Jefferson later became a friend of Burney and had him supervise the building of his daughter Patsy's harpsichord. Robert Carter, as interested in the scientific and mechanical aspects of music as Jefferson, owned and read works on the determination and analysis of pitch, and often performed the experiments described in these works himself.[13]

Americans imported a variety of fine musical instruments and paid high prices for them. As early as the 1730s, "Cremona" violins were awarded as prizes in country fiddling contests. (Many notices of these fiddling and singing contests appear in the *Virginia Gazette*; one of them encouraged attendance by assuring entrants that they would all have "Liquor sufficient to clear their wind-Pipes . . .")[14] Records of the cargoes and destinations of ships leaving Virginia ports noted violins shipped from Virginia to Boston in 1769. These could have been transshipped from Europe or products of Virginia violinmakers. Many merchants offered for sale violins by Cremonese makers, by Jacob Stainer of Absam in the Tyrol, or good copies of Cremona and Stainer violins.

Keyboard instruments were equally ubiquitous. Americans first imported them from England, then turned to building their own. Americans knew that the best harpsichords could be obtained from Plenius of London, and later from either Kirkman or Shudi. In 1767 Benjamin Bucktrout of Williamsburg advertised that he made and repaired spinets and harpsichords, along with "all sorts of Chinese and Gothic Paling for gardens and summer houses."[15] From Bucktrout and others came a long line of skilled American instrument makers, culminating in early nineteenth-century American improvements in pianomaking that became world-famous.[16]

[13] Molnar, pp. 72–73.

[14] Quoted in Stoutamire, pp. 10–11.

[15] *Virginia Gazette*, Jan. 8, 1767.

[16] Molnar, pp. 73–74; Arthur Loesser, *Men, Women, and Pianos* (New York, 1954), p. 463.

Benjamin Franklin wrote down his instructions for building a glass harmonica in 1762. While working on his harmonica, Franklin kept it concealed from his wife until it was ready to play. He surprised her with it by playing it one night when she was asleep. The music awakened her and startled her somewhat—she said she thought it was the music of angels.[17] London craftsmen soon made glass harmonicas commercially. They were well known and very popular throughout the remainder of the century. They cost forty guineas at Longman and Broderip, a London musical instrument manufacturer and music publisher.[18]

Americans also bought large quantities of wind instruments, and all kinds of supplies for caring for them. Newspaper advertisements only hint at the number of instrument purchases, for many people bought them directly from England and thus many instrument sales never appeared in the newspapers.[19]

All things considered, Jefferson must have made his remark about the barbarity of American music in a temporary fit of pique, perhaps after hearing a bad performance. He never appears to have complained again, nor did he really have so much to complain about.

[17] Louis C. Madeira, comp., *Annals of Music in Philadelphia . . .* (Philadelphia, 1896), p. 48.

[18] Loesser, pp. 227–31; A. Hyatt King, "The Musical Glasses and Glass Harmonica," *Proceedings of the Royal Musical Association*, 72 (1946–47): 106–8.

[19] Stoutamire, pp. 16–17, 20.

CHAPTER II

Thomas Jefferson's "Delightful Recreation"

THE VIOLIN, usually called the fiddle, was literally king of instruments in the Virginia of Thomas Jefferson's youth.[1] Keyboard instruments, such as organs, harpsichords, and the new pianofortes, were rarities, although they were beginning to appear in increasing numbers in the homes of rich planters and in closely settled neighborhoods. Fiddles, however, were everywhere; fiddling and singing contests were as much a part of rural social life as were horse racing and athletic events. Whether or not young Thomas Jefferson attended or participated in any of the fiddling contests so frequently advertised in the *Virginia Gazette* remains unknown.

It is impossible to determine when and how young Jefferson learned to play the fiddle or when he got his first one, but we do know that he must have learned while quite young, and that—unlike most of his contemporaries—he did not play solely by ear. Somehow, somewhere, he had had musical instruction that taught him to play correctly by reading music, playing "by book" rather than by "rote or ear."[2] As a child he was not isolated in the backwoods where correct violin instruction was unavailable; by the time he was old enough to receive schooling his family lived at Tuckahoe, where his father was resident executor of the estate of William Randolph and guardian of Randolph's son, Thomas Mann Randolph. After the Jefferson family returned to Shadwell, Peter Jefferson placed his son, aged nine, at the Latin School of the Reverend William Douglas for the next five years. Young Thomas said nothing about music instruction there, and he did not think very highly of Douglas's general ability as a scholar and teacher.[3]

Thomas Jefferson began as a boarding scholar with the Reverend James Maury at fourteen. By that time he was a competent violin player and almost certainly owned an instrument. He copied his favorite country fiddle tunes into music notebooks, sometimes adding

[1] James Parton, "College Days of Thomas Jefferson," *Atlantic Monthly* 29 (1872): 22.

[2] Malone I, 48.

[3] *Ibid.*, pp. 22ff, 39.

lyrics from diverse sources to them. His violin was his favorite indoor amusement at Maury's.[4] During his second year there, John Harvie, his father's executor, paid a Mr. Inglis "for teaching 5 children 6 mo. to dance," in other words, young Thomas and his four sisters. And so he acquired another of the social graces that a young Virginia gentleman would be presumed to possess. A young gentleman, incidentally, learned to play a stringed instrument rather than "puff out the face in a vulgar fashion" with a wind instrument.[5]

Other members of the Jefferson family also showed some aptitude for music. Family tradition says that Thomas's older sister Jane shared both his talent and his enthusiasm for music and that they often practiced playing and singing together. He was particularly fond of hearing her sing old psalm tunes.[6] Randolph Jefferson, Thomas's only brother and his junior by twelve years, played the violin. Thomas, assuming guardianship of Randolph and the other younger children after their father's death, sent Randolph to the College of William and Mary from 1771 to 1773, and noted at least one payment of slightly over six pounds to the violin teacher Alberti for Randolph's violin lessons. It is quite obvious, however, from later letters, that Randolph was not inclined to be scholarly. He settled near Scottsville, Virginia, married "a Jade of genuine bottom,"[7] and seems to have used his musical experience only for country fiddling—"used to come out among the black people, play the fiddle and dance half the night."[8]

Shortly before entering the College of William and Mary early in 1760, young Jefferson met another Virginia fiddler. Jefferson happened to be in Hanover County for the Christmas holidays, staying at the house of Nathaniel Dandridge. Here he met Patrick Henry,

[4] *Ibid.*, pp. 47–48; Randall, I, 18; Edwin Morris Betts, "Jefferson: Gardening and Music," Manuscripts Department, ViU (typescript); Helen D. Bullock, "A Dissertation on Education in the Form of a Letter from James Maury to Robert Jackson, July 17, 1762," *Papers of the Albemarle County Historical Society* 2 (1941–42): 38.

[5] Malone I, 47; Louis B. Wright, *The First Gentlemen of Virginia* (Charlottesville, Va., 1964), p. 10.

[6] Sarah N. Randolph, *The Domestic Life of Thomas Jefferson* (Charlottesville, Va., 1967), p. 34.

[7] Bernard Mayo, ed., *Thomas Jefferson and His Unknown Brother Randolph* (Charlottesville, Va., 1942), pp. 7–8; TJ, Miscellaneous Accounts, 1764–69, May 4, 1774, CSmH; Fee Book and Miscellaneous Accounts, from estate of Peter Jefferson in account with TJ, May 4, 1774, CSmH.

[8] Bernard Mayo, pp. 9–10; Isaac Jefferson, "Memoirs of a Monticello Slave," in *Jefferson at Monticello*, ed. by James A. Bear, Jr. (Charlottesville, Va., 1967), p. 22.

and in the usual holiday open-house atmosphere of Virginia, the two spent a couple of weeks playing the fiddle together and dancing with the rest of the revelers.[9]

Jefferson's entry into Williamsburg society as a college student and later as a young lawyer introduced him to the vigorous musical life of that city and gave him many opportunities as a performer. There he heard the mixture of Italian, French, and German music imported from England. He enjoyed the performances of local professionals, such as Peter Pelham, and visiting theatrical stars. Traveling companies performed English ballad opera and plays with musical interpolation. Gentlemen amateurs and professionals, vocalists, and instrumentalists, performed in the theater, at concerts, and for private entertainment at social functions.[10]

The young red-haired law student, thus exposed for the first time to a great variety of musical experiences, as well as a number of young ladies, must have felt comparatively isolated during the intervals he spent at Shadwell. He confessed to being "vastly pleased" with one young lady's "playing on the spinnette and singing,"[11] and he was most annoyed when rats ate "half a dozen new minuets I had just got, to serve, I suppose as provision for the winter."[12] Through his law mentor, George Wythe, he became a friend of Governor Francis Fauquier, who "was musical also, and a good performer, and associated me with two or three other amateurs in his weekly concerts."[13] Jefferson played violin, of course, and perhaps cello. A fellow violinist and cellist was John Tyler, later governor of Virginia, whose cellist's bow arm Jefferson admired.[14] Governor Fauquier's harpsichordist was Robert Carter of Nomini Hall, from whom Jefferson later tried unsuccessfully to buy an organ.[15] At some time during his Williamsburg years, Jefferson bought a kit, a very small violin used chiefly by dancing masters. He designed and made

[9] TJ, Monticello, to William Wirt, Aug. 5, 1815, quoted in Stan. V. Henkels, "Jefferson's Recollections of Patrick Henry," *Pennsylvania Magazine of History and Biography* 34 (1910): 408; James Parton, p. 25; Jane Carson, *Colonial Virginians at Play* (Williamsburg, Va., 1965), p. 7; Helen D. Bullock, "Mr. Jefferson—Musician," *Etude*, Oct. 1943, p. 634.

[10] For the best descriptions of musical Williamsburg of TJ's time, see: Maurer, "Library of a Colonial Musician," pp. 39–52; Molnar, pp. 63–108.

[11] TJ to William Fleming, Oct. 1763, Boyd I, 12.

[12] TJ to John Page, Dec. 25, 1762, Boyd I, 4.

[13] TJ, Monticello, to L. H. Girardin, Jan. 15, 1815, Lipscomb and Bergh XIV, 232.

[14] Lyon G. Tyler, *Letters and Times of the Tylers* (Richmond, 1884), II, 55.

[15] Malone I, 79; Louis Morton, *Robert Carter of Nomini Hall* (Williamsburg, 1945), pp. 49, 219.

a little case for it that would fit on his saddle and took it with him everywhere. Since its tone was subdued, he could practice on it in his room, wherever he happened to be, without disturbing anyone.[16]

Many account book and ledger entries during the 1760s testify to Jefferson's interest in purchasing musical supplies and attending musical performances. The number of tickets he bought for certain performances indicates that he often took friends to the theater, and certainly those same friends must have reciprocated his invitations. In 1768 he bought a violin in Williamsburg from Dr. William Pasteur, who stocked a variety of drugs, medicines, spices, and sweets, and dealt in musical instruments on the side.[17] He bought fiddle-strings at Hornsby's and at the Printing Office in Williamsburg as well as from a Mr. Richards in Charlottesville.[18]

Practically every theatrical performance he saw involved music. It was the custom of the time to interpolate a somewhat appalling number and variety of musical and dance interludes during and between the acts of plays. The *Virginia Gazette* of May 12, 1768, advertised a program typical of what Jefferson often saw. The main attraction was *The Constant Couple* or *A Trip to the Jubilee*. Between the first and second acts there was to be a "country boy monologue," a dance after the second act, a cantata after the third act, a minuet within the fifth act and a hornpipe after the play. As if this were not already enough of an endurance test for the audience, the advertisement notes: "to which will be added a farce, *The Miller of Mansfield*."[19] Jefferson may have seen this particular performance. He also saw many current ballad operas such as *Love in a Village*, *The Beggar's Opera*, *The Padlock*, and *Thomas and Sally*. In fact he probably saw almost everything performed at the theater while he was in town.[20]

Music was a happily shared mutual interest of Jefferson and his wife, Martha Wayles Skelton Jefferson. Martha played keyboard instruments and guitar. Jefferson's proficiency on the violin and his

16 Randall I, 132; Bullock, "A Dissertation on Education," p. 633.

17 Ledger, 1767–1770, May 25, 1768, CSmH. In the same year Pasteur advertised for sale a two-manual Kirkman harpsichord. *Virginia Gazette*, Nov. 10, 1768, photostat at ViU.

18 Ledger, 1767–1770, Oct. 4 and 13, 1768; Aug. 10, 1769. Account Books, June 23–24, 1770; Oct. 8 and 24, 1770; July 15, 1771.

19 Quoted in Mary N. Stanard, *Colonial Virginia* (Philadelphia, 1917), pp. 242–43.

20 For a complete discussion of performances at Williamsburg, see: Hugh F. Rankin, *The Theater in Colonial America* (Chapel Hill, N.C., 1960); Susan Armstrong, "A Repertoire of the American Colonial Theater," MS. report in Research Department, The Colonial Williamsburg Foundation.

pleasant singing voice were supposedly responsible for helping him eliminate his rivals for the lady's hand.[21] In 1771 he wrote to a London factor to buy a clavichord as a gift for Martha, then, having seen one of the new fortepianos, changed his order to a fortepiano.[22] In the process of settling his father-in-law's estate, Jefferson paid a William Allegre and Frederick Victor twelve pounds for two years of "teaching Mrs. J. on the Spinnet."[23] The years of Jefferson's marriage and his public life in both Williamsburg and Philadelphia show many purchases of musical supplies. He bought music, violin strings, guitar strings, and a violin mute from Michael Hillegas of Philadelphia, and music from Clarkson's in Williamsburg.[24]

Francis Alberti, an immigrant Venetian violinist and harpsichordist, was the man from whom Jefferson, his wife and his brother Randolph took lessons for several years. Alberti was well known to Jefferson and his friends, having taught music for several years in and around Charlottesville.[25] Jefferson said he "got him to come up here [to Charlottesville]" and took lessons from him for several years. He also said that during these years he played his violin "no less than 3 hours a day."[26] Many years later a friend wrote and told Jefferson of Alberti's death in Richmond. The friend had subscribed to Alberti's "band" but had never heard it. Their musical reputation was evidently not of the best—"they surpass in execution, hardly the Jews Harp and Banjer performers."[27]

21 Randolph, *Domestic Life*, p. 44.

22 TJ, Monticello, to Thomas Adams, Feb. 20 and June 1, 1771, Boyd I, 62, 71–72.

23 Miscellaneous Accounts, 1764–69, July 13, 1772; Fee Book and Miscellaneous Accounts, July 13, 1772, CSmH.

24 Account Books, June 22, July 28, Oct. 16, 1775; May 24, Aug. 31, 1776; May 26, 1779. Michael Hillegas operated a music shop at his house on Second Street in Philadelphia, 1759–65. He is later listed as a Philadelphia music publisher, ca. 1776. He was one of the gifted amateur performers of Francis Hopkinson's circle and was also Treasurer of the Pennsylvania Committee of Safety. William A. Fisher, *One Hundred and Fifty Years of Music Publishing in the United States, 1783–1933* (Boston, 1933), p. 23; Oscar G. Sonneck, *A Bibliography of Early American Secular Music*, revised and enlarged by William T. Upton (Washington, D.C., 1945), p. 579; George E. Hastings, *The Life and Works of Francis Hopkinson* (Chicago, 1926), p. 276. Clarkson and Davis published the *Virginia Gazette*, 1779–80.

25 Account Books, Mar. 20, 1772; Ledger, 1767–1770, Mar. 23, 1768, CSmH; Malone I, 159.

26 Nicholas Trist, Memorandum of Mar. 22, 1826, NPT, DLC.

27 James Currie, Richmond, to TJ, Paris, Aug. 5, 1785, Boyd VIII, 342. There was one form of local music which Alberti did not appreciate at all. Some friends once took him for a fox hunt. When the hounds were in full cry, the men asked Alberti how he liked the music. Alberti replied that "de dam

Several paroled British and German officers settled temporarily near Charlottesville early in 1779 after the Battle of Saratoga. The musicians among them soon became regular visitors at Monticello. An English officer who was aide-de-camp to General Simon Fraser spoke of many musical evenings at Monticello. A violinist himself, the Englishman lavishly praised Jefferson's skill on that instrument.[28] Major General Friederich Adolph, Baron von Riedesel, moved his wife and daughters into the neighboring estate of Colle. The baroness had a beautiful soprano voice, although reputedly loud enough to drown out the pianoforte accompaniment sometimes furnished by Mrs. Jefferson.[29] A German officer describing the Jefferson household in a Hamburg newspaper said that Jefferson had an "Elegant Harpsichord Piano forte and some Violins." He had a high opinion of Jefferson's skill on the violin and Martha's skill on the keyboard. A friend sent Jefferson the newspaper clippings.[30]

Jefferson's best friend among the Germans was a Captain Baron von Geismar, another violinist. Geismar, the only son of a seventy-year-old father, wanted very badly to be exchanged or allowed to go home on parole to look after his family's estates. Jefferson intervened on his behalf, writing to Richard Henry Lee, the Virginia delegate to Congress, to explain the circumstances. Lee promised to do as much as possible to expedite matters, although the British created difficulties about paroles. Many months later, Geismar was in New York, still waiting for his parole, thanking the Jeffersons for their kindness and sending special greetings to "my little friend Paty [*sic*]." Eventually Jefferson heard from Riedesel that Geismar was on his way home after almost a year and a half of waiting. Geismar left all of his music for Jefferson.[31] Jefferson corresponded with Geismar until 1789. The two friends enjoyed a four-day reunion in the Rhineland in April 1788.[32]

Following his wife's death in 1782, Jefferson accepted the position

---

dog make such a noise me no hear de music." Sarah N. Randolph, unpublished and untitled manuscript, EHR, ViU; Sarah N. Randolph, "Mrs. Thomas Mann Randolph," in *Worthy Women of Our First Century*, ed. Mrs. O. J. Wister and Agnes Irwin (Philadelphia, 1877), p. 56.

[28] Randall I, 132–33.

[29] Marie Kimball, *Jefferson: War and Peace, 1776 to 1784* (New York, 1947), p. 36.

[30] Jacob Rubsamen to TJ, Dec. 1, 1780, Boyd IV, 174.

[31] TJ, Monticello, to Richard Henry Lee, Philadelphia, Apr. 21, 1779, Boyd II, 225; Lee to TJ, May 22, 1779, *ibid.*, 270; Geismar, New York, to TJ, Monticello, Feb. 26, 1780, Boyd III, 304; Riedesel, New York, to TJ, Monticello, Oct. 2, 1780, Boyd IV, 4, 173.

[32] Kimball, pp. 41–45; Malone I, 295.

of minister plenipotentiary for negotiating peace when Congress offered him the position. He then made plans to leave for Europe. He left his two younger children, Maria (Polly) and Lucy, with their maternal aunt, Mrs. Francis Eppes, at Eppington and took his eleven-year-old daughter Martha (Patsy) north with him. Ice and the presence of British warships in the Baltimore harbor prevented him from leaving as scheduled, and Congress withdrew the appointment. In the meantime the Virginia House of Delegates elected him to Congress. He arrived in Philadelphia in December 1782 and settled down to several months of congressional service, interspersed with visits to Monticello. He placed Patsy in the care of Mrs. Thomas Hopkinson of Philadelphia, widowed mother of his musical friend Francis Hopkinson, a fellow signer of the Declaration of Independence.[33] He paid three pounds entrance money and three pounds monthly thereafter for Patsy's music lessons with John Bentley. He enrolled her with a dancing master, rented a clavichord for her to practice on, and had his own violin repaired.[34]

Any music-loving resident of Philadelphia during the 1780s and well into the nineteenth century could be assured of hearing good music. On November 6, 1783, the following advertisement appeared in the *Pennsylvania Packet*:

City Concert

The subscribers will please to take notice that the next concert will be on Tuesday the 11th instant, at the Lodge Room. As a number of gentlemen expressed a desire of subscription, whose subscriptions Mr. Bentley could not receive until he had ascertained the number the room would hold: he now informs them that the subscription is open for 25 more subscribers, after which it will be finally closed. Tickets for non-subscribers may be had at 10s each.

The Mr. Bentley mentioned was John Bentley, English harpsichordist recently come to America and founder of this fortnightly series of city concerts, which he presented for two years. There were eleven concerts in this first series, and they continued from October 1783 to early April 1784. Unfortunately the newspaper did not print the programs of these concerts or the names of the performers. Bentley had a reputation as a fine musician, undoubtedly engaged the best available talent, and performed music in keeping with the tastes of Hopkinson and Jefferson;[35] Jefferson, however, heard better performances in Philadelphia than in Williamsburg. There is no

[33] Randolph, *Domestic Life*, pp. 67–68; Malone I, 339–400.
[34] Account Books, Nov. 17–21, 1783.
[35] Sonneck, *Concert Life*, pp. 78–79.

doubt that Patsy, in having Bentley for her music teacher, had the best teacher available. Jefferson bought a nonsubscription ticket for the concert held on November 11, 1783.[36] He may have attended some of the others as a guest.

The two Jeffersons, father and elder daughter, finally reached France in August 1784.[37] Jefferson's new appointment was to assist John Adams and Benjamin Franklin in obtaining advantageous commercial treaties.[38] An old friend, Philip Mazzei, sent Jefferson some memoranda before he left, concerning persons whom he would want to contact. Above all, said Mazzei, Jefferson would want to make the acquaintance of the musicians Piccini and Caravoglia. Knowing Piccini would enable Jefferson to hear "now and then some pieces of divine musick in private, which has ever done me greater pleasure than anything of the kind done in public." Caravoglia was particularly good on the German flute. He was also "very modest, and more sensible than that Sort of People generally are, he don't show it on account of his eternal Silence. I think he is the very Person Mr. Jefferson will want to play with him."[39] Jefferson did become friendly with Piccini, and even asked him for advice about ordering Patsy's harpsichord. The new minister was exhilarated by his exposure to the great European traditions in the fine arts, especially music. He envied the French their music, saying that he coveted it "in spite of all the authority of the Decalogue."[40] And how easy for a violin lover to covet the music of France, especially since he was in the middle of the best period of French violin music—a blending of the French techniques with those of Italy and Germany, and a period of the "perfect trinity" of violin composers, performers, and makers.[41]

Jefferson took full advantage of everything musical that Paris had to offer. He bought violin and guitar strings, music stands and desks, a small violin, a guitar, a bird organ, and stacks of music. He rented a piano for two years for Patsy, then ordered her a splendid Kirkman

[36] Account Books, Nov. 12, 1783.

[37] Polly (Maria) Jefferson and Lucy Jefferson, the other two daughters, remained in the care of their maternal aunt, Mrs. Francis (Elizabeth) Eppes, at Eppington. Lucy died there of whooping cough in the fall of 1784. Randolph, *Domestic Life*, p. 101.

[38] Malone II, 3.

[39] Philip Mazzei's Memoranda Regarding Persons and Affairs in Paris [ca. July, 1784], Boyd VII, 388–89.

[40] TJ, Paris, to Charles Bellini, Sept. 30, 1785, Boyd VIII, 659.

[41] For the best account of the history of violins and violin playing in Europe in Jefferson's time, see David Boyden, *The History of Violin Playing from its Origins to 1761 and its Relationship to the Violin and Violin Music* (London, 1965).

harpsichord from London (see Chapter IV). When his younger daughter, Polly, joined them, he enrolled both girls with a harpsichord teacher, a guitar master, and a dancing master.[42] In Paris and during his European travels he went to every imaginable kind of musical performance—opera, concerts, private home musical evenings and mixtures of music and spectacle similar to what he had seen in Williamsburg. He was a regular frequenter of the Concerts Spirituels, a Paris institution, held in the Tuileries. Originally their purpose was to provide music on holy days, when opera performances were prohibited, but by the time of Jefferson's visit they were almost entirely secular in nature.[43]

Jefferson, the amateur, heard many of the best violinists and much of the best violin music of the day at these concerts and at the opera. He heard Giovanni Battista Viotti, the greatest of them all, many times,[44] and heard Viotti's compositions performed by other violinists. He heard Rodolphe Kreutzer, whom many contemporaries ranked with Viotti. He heard Viotti's pupils, Paul Alday and Madame Gautherot. He was already familiar with the violin music of Luigi Boccherini and Carlo Antonio Campioni, whose compositions had been the rage of Paris in the 1760s. He went to benefit performances for the violinists Madam Gautherot, Johann Frederick Eck, and George Bridgetower.

The latter represents a type of performer common in the Paris of the 1780s—the child prodigy. Bridgetower was a mulatto boy who later became famous all over Europe and eventually played duets with Beethoven. Jefferson must have heard one of Bridgetower's earliest performances, if not the first; he bought tickets for a benefit concert by the nine-year-old boy, which was held on May 27, 1789. Bridgetower played compositions by Viotti, Groffe, and Jarnowick (Giornovichi). Jefferson heard Mademoiselle Rose Renaud sing many times both in concerts and at the opera, and occasionally he heard her sister Sophie. Mlle. Rose was only sixteen when he heard her in *Penelope*, by Piccini and Marmontel, and commented to Abigail Adams on what a fine singer she was.[45] On May 10, 1786, he bought tickets for a benefit concert by the Descarsin sisters—Sophie,

[42] Account Books, Nov. 30, 1784; Jan. 24, Mar. 3 and 7, Aug. 15, Sept. 28, 1785; Jan. 27, Aug. 15, Oct. 13, 1788; Sept. 19 and 24, Oct. 4, 1789.

[43] Loesser, pp. 311–13. All of the information on performances TJ saw comes from the *Journal de Paris* and *The London Chronicle for 1786*. Information on individual performers and composers is from the Grove and Fétis dictionaries (see Bibliography).

[44] Trist, Memorandum.

[45] TJ, Paris, to Abigail Adams, Dec. 27, 1785, Boyd IX, 126.

aged seven, and Caroline, aged twelve—who played harp compositions by Cardon, Krumpholtz, LaManière, and Petrini, and Caroline played a composition of her own. He also heard the debut of fourteen-year-old Joseph François Narcisse Carbonel, who sang his own composition, "Ode on the Death of Duke Leopold of Brunswick." Young Carbonel, after this beginning, does not appear on other concert programs.

Jefferson heard many of the most famous performers and composers of his day—cellists, horn players, bass players, flautists, clarinetists, and keyboard artists. He heard singers who sang at the opera and had international reputations, having toured Europe and England. Two of the most famous women singers he heard were Madame Gertrud Elisabeth Mara and Madame Luiza Todi, known as bitter rivals as well as competent singers. He attended many operas by André Ernest Grétry, and others by Antonio Sacchini, Egidio Duni, Nicholas Dezède, Niccolo Piccini, Nicholas Dalayrac, and Pierre Monsigny. He heard the music of Karl Friedrich Abel, Johann Friedrich Edelman, Jean Davaux, Leopold Kozeluch, Josef Myslivecek, and Johann Sterkel—all unknown today but as famous in their time as their contemporaries, Handel, Haydn, Mozart, and C. P. E. Bach are today. Jefferson, of course, was also familiar with these last four giants and had a considerable collection of their music.

Jefferson retained a fondness for the kind of music-plus-spectacle extravaganzas that he had seen in Williamsburg. In Paris he bought tickets to Jean Baptiste Nicolet's vaudeville entertainments, where he saw tightrope acts, farce, pantomimes, and juggling, liberally interspersed with musical acts. In London he went to Sadler's Wells and saw *The Restoration of Hymen*, which, from its newspaper description, must have been spectacular. It combined music, mythology, Harlequin and Colombine, clowns, and scenery in an enormous "New Pantomime."

The artist John Trumbull introduced Jefferson to many of his friends, among them the artists Richard and Maria Cosway. Mrs. Cosway, in addition to being an artist, was a talented singer, harpist, pianist, and composer. For a month or so after their first meeting, and before the Cosways returned to England, Jefferson and Maria spent part of nearly every day together, enjoying the best of Parisian art, architecture, and music. They visited Johann Krumpholtz, one of the most outstanding of several teachers and composers for the harp in Paris. They probably attended concerts and the opera together, or in a party of friends. Shortly after Maria left Paris in October 1786, Jefferson sent her a copy of "Jour heureux," a favorite air from Sacchini's opera *Dardanus*. His account book does not mention tickets for the performance of this opera on October 3, 1786, but it is possible that he and Maria saw it together as guests of some of their friends. While Maria was in England they corresponded, he with his head once more in control of his heart and she somewhat vexed with the restraint and infrequency of his letters. They saw each other only occasionally on her other visits to Paris, and they corresponded sporadically throughout the rest of Jefferson's life.[46]

When Jefferson went to Philadelphia after his return from France, he went to a city where he could hear some very good music, possibly the best he could hear anywhere in English-speaking America and on a par with much that he had heard in Europe. Alexander Reinagle, an English harpsichordist, conductor, and composer, had settled in Philadelphia and become prominent as a music teacher, performer, and conductor. He conducted and played harpsichord for opera orchestras in several other cities in addition to Philadelphia. Besides Reinagle, there were Henry Capron and John Christopher Moller. Capron, a composer, cellist, guitarist, and singer, had been one of the Philadelphia City Concert managers while Jefferson was in France and had by 1792 returned to Philadelphia from a short period of residence in New York. Moller was a composer, organist, pianist, harpsichordist, and publisher who also came to Philadelphia from New York. In Philadelphia he was organist at Zion Church, teacher and performer, harmonica specialist, and music teacher to young Polly Jefferson.[47]

Moller, Capron, and Reinagle assumed direction of the Philadelphia City Concerts for the winter of 1792–93. They advertised the concert series in Bache's *General Advertiser* in October 1792:

CITY CONCERT of Vocal and Instrumental Music under the direction of Messrs. Reinagle, Moller and Capron. The principal vocal part by Mrs. Hodgkinson. The public are respectfully informed the first concert will be held on Saturday the 18th day of November at Oeller's Hotel in Chestnutstreet [*sic*]. The directors flatter themselves that from the engagements they have made with the several performers of eminence, and the arrangements of the music, the concerts will meet with the approbation of the public.[48]

Mr. Oellers received subscriptions for the concert series at his hotel. Jefferson bought a subscription from Oellers for both the concert

[46] Malone II, 70–81; Helen D. Bullock, *My Head and My Heart* (New York, 1945), pp. 13–28.

[47] Sonneck, *Bibliography*, pp. 501, 517, 521. Account Books, Oct. 31, Nov. 8, 1792; Apr. 14, 1793.

[48] Quoted in Sonneck, *Concert Life*, p. 87.

series and a series of dancing assemblies.[49] The first concert was held on December 1, 1792, having been postponed from November 18. The series followed thereafter on December 15 and December 29, 1792, and January 12, January 26, February 9, March 2 and March 31, 1793. Jefferson was in Philadelphia on all of these dates and could have attended the entire series.[50]

At these concerts he heard good chamber music performed by capable musicians. He had already bought music by many of the composers featured in the concert programs for his own music library. Moller, Capron, and Reingale themselves performed most of the music, assisted by Moller's daughter and various other local "performers of eminence." The programs featured the works of J. C. Bach, Haydn, Pelissier, Stamitz, Kozeluch, Abel, Martini, Boccherini, Pleyel, and the three impresarios, performed on the piano, cello, bassoon, clarinet, flute, horn, and violin, and many combinations of these instruments.[51]

Later residence in Philadelphia in the waning years of the century contain no references to concert attendance at all, and only one subscription to a dancing assembly. Shortly before and after his last stay in Philadelphia, Jefferson took dancing lessons from "Vaughan the dancing master" in Charlottesville—an interesting bit of information, but with no purchases of dancing assembly memberships to account for the lessons.[52]

The Washington of Thomas Jefferson's years as President wanted "nothing . . . but houses, cellars, kitchens, well-informed men, amiable women, and other trifles of the sort to make our city perfect."[53] Foreign visitors as well as Americans complained about Washington's primitive conditions. The poet Thomas Moore, whose dislike of Jefferson and the United States colored his verse, nevertheless expressed the general opinion of many people toward the city of Washington:

> Where tribunes rule, where dusky Davi bow,
> And what was Goose Creek once is Tiber now:
> This embryo capital, where Fancy sees

[49] Account Books, Nov. 27, 1792.

[50] Sonneck, *Concert Life*, pp. 87–91; James A. Bear, Jr., Chronology (typescript; see Bibliography), Monticello Archives, Monticello.

[51] Sonneck, *Concert Life*, pp. 87–91.

[52] Account Books, Feb. 1 and 2, 1798; Oct. 21, 1799; July 22, 1800.

[53] Gouverneur Morris, quoted in Maude G. Sewall, "Washington and Its Musical History," *Music Teachers National Association, Proceedings*, 27th Series (1932), p. 35.

Squares in morasses, obelisks in trees;
Where second-sighted seers e'en now adorn
With shrines unbuilt and heroes yet unborn
Though now but woods—and Jefferson—they see
Where streets should run and sages ought to be.[54]

Music lovers were really lost in Washington. They had to depend on Philadelphia for all musical merchandise until about 1804. There was a "miserable little rope-walking theater,"[55] where the Philadelphia Company sometimes came on tour, and there were dancing assemblies and public dinners. The Philadelphia Company, managed by Alexander Reinagle and Thomas Wignell, did a little of everything. They were a large group, often numbering as many as seventy persons, with a twenty-piece orchestra. They mounted operatic and dramatic productions, sometimes abbreviating the plays to fit musical acts into them. Another form of dramatic entertainment was the vaudeville potpourri of acts and music that Jefferson always liked to see whenever he had a chance.[56]

And then there was the Marine Band. It is difficult to sort out the true story of the Marine Band from all of the tales surrounding its origin, and there is serious doubt as to whether or not Jefferson had as much to do with it as some writers of articles seem to think. He supported either the Marine Band or an unnamed "Musick Band" with occasional gifts of cash, and he encouraged anything that led to improvement in their performances.

The Marine Band had been organized in Washington in 1800 at the suggestion of Colonel William Ward Burrows, first commandant of the United States Marine Corps. He further suggested that the corps enlist boys specifically as musicians, and train them as fifers and drummers. There was even a "Music Fund," which consisted of subscriptions by the officers and which was used to buy instruments and pay bounties for enlisting "musics." Whatever fifes and drums they had to begin with, they augmented in August 1808 by purchasing two French horns, two C clarinets, one bassoon, one bass drum, as well as reeds and supplies for the instruments. From May to November they gave outdoor concerts on Saturday afternoons, often on the grounds around the President's House. They

[54] Quoted in Constance M. Green, *Washington, Village and Capitol, 1800–1878* (Princeton, 1962), I, 38–39.

[55] *Ibid.*, p. 45.

[56] *Ibid.* For an excellent short discussion of music in Washington from 1800 to 1812, see John C. Haskins, "Music in the District of Columbia, 1800 to 1814" (M.A. thesis, Catholic University, 1952).

played for a dancing assembly at Stelle's Hotel and at President Adams's New Year's Day reception.[57]

Reports of their skill vary. A Marine Band historian says that they played at Thomas Jefferson's inauguration on March 4, 1801. They played "with great precision and with inspiring animation the *President's March*" and other patriotic and martial airs at the Fourth of July celebration, 1801. As their fame spread, they were asked to play at private affairs, for which they charged fifty dollars and expenses.[58] They did not, however, do so well at Sunday services in the Hall of Representatives. According to Mrs. Samuel Harrison Smith: "The musick was as little in union with devotional feelings as the place. The Marine Band, were the performers. Their scarlet uniform, their various instruments, made quite a dazzling appearance in the gallery. The marches they played were good and inspiring, but in their attempts to accompany the psalm-singing of the congregation, they completely failed and after a while, the practice was discontinued—it was *too* ridiculous."[59]

Jefferson enters the story of the Marine Band through that old enemy of the historian, tradition. Tradition says that he and Colonel Burrows went out horseback riding one day and discussed, among other things, the Marine Band. Jefferson thought that they were pretty bad and supposedly suggested enlisting some musicians in Italy as Marines and bringing them back either as a new band or to augment the existing one. Wherever the idea came from, Burrows, in 1803, told Captain John Hall, who was with Commander Edward Preble's squadron in the Mediterranean, to enlist the Italians. Hall enlisted eighteen Italians and bought instruments, much to the consternation of Colonel Burrows's successor, who knew nothing of any such orders. The Italians and their families arrived in Washington on September 19, 1805. They were not impressed—their "captain," Gaetano Caruso, said that they "arrived in a desert; in fact a place containing some two or three taverns, with a few scattering cottages or log huts, called the City of Washington, the Me-

[57] Green, I, 18, 46; Wilhelmus B. Bryan, *A History of the National Capital* (New York, 1914), I, p. 371; Major Edwin North McClellan, "The U.S. Marine Band," Music Division, DLC (typescript); Major Edwin North McClellan, "How the Marine Band Started," *U.S. Institute Proceedings*, 49 (Apr. 1923): 581–86; John Clagett Proctor, "Marine Band History and Its Leaders," Magazine Section, *Washington Sunday Star*, May 8, 1932, pp. 6ff.

[58] McClellan, "How the Marine Band Started."

[59] Galliard Hunt, ed., *The First Forty Years of Washington Society: in the Family Letters of Margaret Bayard Smith* (New York, 1965), pp. 13–14.

tropolis of the United States of America."[60] It is not clear whether they were a separate band or were added to the original one. Eventually all but six of them resigned from the corps, but several future leaders of the band came from the remaining six and their families.[61]

Beginning in 1805, Jefferson notes in his account books an annual payment of twenty or thirty dollars to either the "Marine Band" or the "Music Band."[62] It is not clear whether these two are the same group, or exactly why Jefferson gave them money. The most reasonable explanation is that he was paying them for playing at the customary New Year's Day reception at the President's House. Several of these receptions were written up in the *National Intelligencer* and they usually mention "pieces of instrumental music played at intervals" for the "large concourse of individuals."[63]

While in Washington, Jefferson also paid for memberships in three dancing assemblies: the Washington Dancing Assembly, the Georgetown Dancing Assembly, and the Dancing Assemblies organized by Pontius D. Stelle at his hotel.[64] We do not know whether he actually attended any of these assemblies or whether he simply contributed to their support. Since his daughter Martha Randolph and her children visited him during the winter of 1805–6, it is possible that her oldest daughter, Anne Cary Randolph, attended some of these assemblies. Jefferson bought theater tickets twice during Martha's visit. One performance was a triple bill of the comedy *Midnight Hour*, the farce *Lovers Quarrels*, and the pantomime *The Death of Captain Cook*. The other was the comedy *I'll Tell You What* and the pantomime *Don Juan*.[65] Jefferson's only other Washington theater ticket purchase was for one of his old favorites, a spectacle. He bought tickets for Signor Manfredi's "rope-walking"show, which featured all sorts of musical and nonmusical tightrope acts, including a Spanish fandango danced over eggs by Manfredi himself.[66]

[60] McClellan, "How the Marine Band Started."

[61] Green, p. 46; Proctor; McClellan.

[62] Account Books, Jan. 2, 1805; Jan. 8, 1806; Jan. 7, 1807; Jan. 5, 1808; Jan. 11, 1809.

[63] *National Intelligencer*, Jan. 4, 1808; Jan. 4, 1809. For Jefferson's last New Year's Day he wore a suit of homespun and the newspaper reported that the idea of his retirement was "pathetic and solemn."

[64] Account Books, Nov. 27 and Dec. 2, 1801; Dec. 16, 1802; Jan. 11, May 5, Nov. 23, 1805; Feb. 27, 1806; Jan. 17, 1807; Jan. 4, 1808.

[65] Account Books, Dec. 14 and 18, 1805; *National Intelligencer*, Dec. 13 and 17, 1805.

[66] Account Books, Dec. 22, 1806; *National Intelligencer*, Dec. 22, 1806. For the comfort of the audience, there were to be stoves in the theater and no one was to smoke "segars."

In March 1809 Jefferson left public life to return to Monticello and, in the words of Mrs. Samuel H. Smith, he went "to be *happy* without ceasing to be *great*."[67] He was indeed happy to get back to the business of running Monticello, surrounded by his family. Family correspondence indicates that he did not now play the violin much, but we know that he continued to take a lively interest in the musical education of his granddaughters (see Chapter III).

The great project of his last years was the University of Virginia. Scattered through the voluminous amount of material concerning the university, we find several indications of Jefferson's belief that musical training should be available. In an early plan for a school system, which he outlined in a letter to Peter Carr in 1814, he noted three levels of schools: elementary, general, and professional. He named fine arts as one division of the professional level, and it was to include civil architecture, gardening, painting, sculpture, and theory of music.[68] He carried these general ideas over into his plans for the university—a room in the Rotunda, or principal building of the university, was to be reserved for "instruction in drawing, music, or any other of the innocent and ornamental accomplishments of life."[69] Furthermore, students, although they were not to make unduly disturbing noises, would be told that the "proper use of musical instruments shall be freely allowed in their rooms, and in that appropriated for instruction in music."[70] Eventually, music theory would be added to the curriculum.[71] In 1825 the university advertised in Richmond, Philadelphia, and New York for a music teacher, "a good practical performer on more than one instrument, and well versed in orchestral performance and the science of composition."[72] They had difficulty filling the position because it was not salaried; the music teacher only got fees for lessons. The university did not get a music teacher until 1828, and even then he still only got lesson fees.[73]

One very persistent prospective faculty member wrote several times to Jefferson, applying for a job at the university and obviously not taking the hint that he was not wanted. This was David Mariano, an Italian, who in August 1819 stated that he had been in this country for eighteen months. He taught languages at Transylvania Univer-

67 Hunt, p. 58.

68 TJ to Peter Carr, Sept. 7, 1814, Lipscomb and Bergh XIX, 211–21.

69 Lipscomb and Bergh XIX, 450.

70 *Ibid.*, 446.

71 Philip Alexander Bruce, *History of the University of Virginia 1819–1919* (New York, 1922), I, 262, 330.

72 *Ibid.*, II, 126.

73 *Ibid.*, pp. 126–27.

sity in Lexington, Kentucky, and wished to apply for the same position at the new University of Virginia. He also wanted to teach music, having taught it in Philadelphia. After saying that he could teach music "in all its branches," he added that he would teach piano, as he was "quite ignorant of any other [instrument]." He ranted against Americans who, he said, considered music a "mechanical art" and did not teach it properly. He pointed out that Italians felt differently about it. He sent a literary journal that he and another professor had edited to demonstrate additional abilities. Jefferson wrote and told him that present university funds were going for accommodations, and professors would not be nominated until after that. Mariano, undaunted, wrote again in November 1820 renewing his request and asking to know what his duties would be if hired. Jefferson replied curtly that the opening of the university depended on aid from the legislature, and thus he could not answer Mariano's inquiries.[74] A memo in Jefferson's handwriting, of Thomas Sully's opinion of Mariano might be a further reason for Jefferson's lack of enthusiasm: "Mariano—Mr. Sully speaks very favorably. He understands Fr[ench] Ital[ian] Span[ish] one of the two last is his native tongue. has been in America 2 or 3 years—speaks English fluently and correctly. genteel, good humored, correct. perhaps a little salacious. 40 y. old. single."[75]

Mr. Jefferson selected books for the University of Virginia library and arranged for their purchase. He included works on music history for the section devoted to fine arts. In 1825 he made a catalogue of the books he thought necessary for the library, arranging it as he did the catalogue of his own library. The volumes that he listed were also in his own library. For the university library, he ordered the following books on music:

1. Arteaga, Esteban. *La Rivoluzioni de Teatro Musicale Italiano.* Bologna, 1783–88. This work comprised three volumes. Jefferson ordered all three, but the university only received two. Jefferson's own set of this work is now in the Library of Congress.
2. Burney, Charles. *The Present State of Music in France and Italy.* The university did not receive this book. Jefferson's copy went to the Library of Congress.
3. Burney, Charles. *The Present State of Music in Germany, the Nether-*

[74] David Mariano, Lexington, to TJ, Monticello, Aug. 7, 1819, TJ Papers, ViU; Mariano to TJ, Nov. 22, 1819, DLC; TJ to Mariano, Sept. 10, 1819, TJ Papers, ViU; Mariano to TJ, Nov. 26, 1820, TJ Papers, ViU; TJ to Mariano, Dec. 28, 1820, TJ Papers, ViU.

[75] TJ Memorandum on David Mariano [1821?], TJ Papers, ViU.

lands, and United Provinces . . . in two volumes. The university never got this work either, and again, Jefferson's copy went to the Library of Congress.

Jefferson also ordered the two *Musique* volumes and several other volumes of the *Encyclopédie Méthodique* published in Paris by Panckoucke, 1782–1816.[76]

As stated earlier, one room of the Rotunda was to be reserved for private individuals to use to teach music, drawing, and dancing. One person who wished to teach dancing and fencing there was a Mr. Xaupi, who numbered some of Jefferson's younger grandchildren among his pupils. In August 1825 Xaupi learned that he might not be allowed to continue to teach fencing. He had nine dancing students and ten fencing students, who were always in "perfect order," and he wanted to be reassured that he could keep them.[77] Jefferson wrote back that the teaching of dancing was perfectly acceptable—the Board of Visitors provided the room for the teaching of music, drawing, "or any other of the *innocent* and ornamental accomplishments of life.

"Dancing [Jefferson continued] is generally, and justly, I think, considered among *innocent* accomplishments; while we cannot so consider the art of stabbing and pistolling our friends, or dexterity in the practice of an instrument exclusively used for killing our fellow-citizens *only* and never against the public enemy."[78] Xaupi could certainly have the room when the Rotunda was finished, but only for teaching the "*innocent*" accomplishment.

Thus Jefferson spent his last years at Monticello, "very active, lively, and happy, riding from 10 to 15 miles every day, and talking without the least restraint, very pleasantly, upon all subjects . . . Mr. Jefferson seems to enjoy life highly, and very rationally."[79]

[76] William B. O'Neal, *Jefferson's Fine Arts Library for the University of Virginia* (Charlottesville, Va., 1956). The *Encyclopédie* was completed in 1832, with 166½ volumes. Jefferson's own set, comprising 136½ volumes, went to DLC.

[77] Xaupi, Charlottesville, to TJ, Monticello, Aug. 31, 1825, DLC.

[78] TJ to Xaupi, Sept. 1, 1825, DLC.

[79] O. W. Long, *Thomas Jefferson and George Ticknor: A Chapter in American Scholarship* (Williamstown, Mass., 1933), pp. 34–35.

CHAPTER III

The Musical Education of Daughters and Granddaughters

THOMAS JEFFERSON once wrote to a friend to thank him for recommending a French tutor for his daughter Patsy, and in one pithy sentence he expressed his reason for his close supervision of the education of daughters, and later, granddaughters. Predicting Patsy's probable future, he lamented that "the chance that in marriage she will draw a blockhead I calculate to about fourteen to one, and of course that the education of her family will probably rest on her ideas and direction without assistance."[1] Besides being able to educate her children to Jefferson's standards, Patsy was also supposed to know and perform faultlessly all the tasks of running an eighteenth-century household. It never occurred to Jefferson that the former might possibly make an intelligent young woman frustrated and dissatisfied with the latter. Abby Adams, daughter of John Adams, was more sanguine about the situation. She thought Jefferson might regret that he gave Patsy and Polly the kind of education that he did. It was quite suitable for them while they were in France, but how could they be happy, or more important, find the right men, when they returned to the United States? Abby thought that if their mother were still alive things would be different.[2]

"Music, drawing, books, invention and exercise will be so many resources to you against ennui," wrote Papa to fifteen-year-old Patsy.[3] He went on at great length in a letter that, by today's standards, is preachy and even a little cold to delineate exactly what he expected of two girls not really old enough to cope with such a program. He suspected that Patsy did not work as hard as he wished. For her own good, she must avoid indolence and idleness. Physical exercise, too, was necessary. Her American character could overcome any obstacle; therefore, if she really tried, she could read her hated Livy. Furthermore, she was to learn sewing and "domestic economy." He promised to write her the long letters she wanted on condition

[1] TJ, Annapolis, to the Marquis de Marbois, Dec. 5, 1783, Boyd IV, 374.

[2] Katherine M. Roof, *Colonel William Smith and Lady* (Boston, 1929), p. 153.

[3] TJ, Aix-en-Provence, to Martha Jefferson, Paris, Mar. 28, 1787, Boyd XI, 251.

that she read them several times and practice what he wished: "My expectations from you are high: yet not higher than you may attain. Industry and resolution are all that are wanting. No body in this world can make me so happy, or so miserable as you. Retirement from public life will ere long become necessary for me. To your sister and yourself I look to render the evening of my life serene and contented. It's [*sic*] morning has been clouded by loss after loss till I have nothing left but you."[4] Great exertions were necessary, but Patsy could be what he wanted her to be. He told her these things because he loved her and knew perfectly what her life would be like, and he wanted her "more qualified than common."[5] Patsy assured him that she would live up to his expectations, "for what I hold most precious is your satisfaction, indeed I should be miserable without it."[6] Somehow the child held on to her sense of humor and twitted him for using such wide margins in his long letter.

Music was naturally an important part of both girls' education. Unlike most girls of their era, their music studies did not "droop sharply after the mating season,"[7] especially Patsy's. Dancing went along with music. In 1779, when Patsy was seven years old, her father enrolled her for dancing lessons with Mrs. Sarah Hallam of Williamsburg. He spent about seventy-five pounds on her dancing lessons over the next six months.[8]

After her mother's death in 1782 Patsy became her father's inseparable companion. Father and daughter set out for Philadelphia, where he entered congressional service and she was settled in the care of Mrs. Thomas Hopkinson, the widowed mother of Jefferson's friend, Francis Hopkinson.[9] While her father followed Congress to Annapolis, Patsy "danced out the old year" with the Hopkinson and Rittenhouse children.[10] Jefferson, always anxious about her education, sent her a formidable daily schedule, which included three

[4] *Ibid.*, 251–52.

[5] *Ibid.*

[6] Martha Jefferson, Paris, to TJ, [Aix-en-Provence], Apr. 9, 1787, Boyd XI, 282.

[7] Loesser, p. 457.

[8] Account Books, Oct. 15, 1779; Jan. 15 and Apr. 7, 1780. Sarah Hallam was the wife of Lewis Hallam, Jr., of the Virginia Company of Comedians. She was not much of an actress, having only appeared on stage once, and in a minor part. Hallam abandoned her and she settled in Williamsburg, ca. 1762. She may have operated a boarding house ca. 1770, and she opened her dancing school in August 1775. She was prosperous, well-known, respected, and popular among the ladies of Williamsburg. Rankin, pp. 198–99, 247.

[9] Randolph, *Domestic Life*, pp. 67–68; Malone I, 399–400.

[10] Hastings, p. 334.

hours of music practice and literally left her no time to eat.[11] She had dancing lessons from Conas the dancing master, she had a rented clavichord to practice on, and she had keyboard lessons with John Bentley, one of the best musicians in Philadelphia (see Chapter II).[12] She was probably quite accomplished at both dancing and the keyboard. Her drawing teacher, Pierre Eugène du Simitière, gave up in disgust, however, saying that he was not a schoolmaster and thus not obliged to teach "those who have no capacity." Hopkinson thought this unjust and told Jefferson not to pay him.[13]

Arrival in Paris in 1784 meant that daughter as well as father was exposed to more opportunities for hearing and studying good music. The harpsichord instructor at the Abbaye Royale de Panthémont, Patsy's school in Paris, was Claude Balbastre, organist of the Church of St. Roch and recognized as one of the foremost organists and harpsichordists in France.[14] Patsy's father rented a pianoforte for her to practice on and undoubtedly to accompany his violin playing, when she visited him at home. During her father's travels she kept him informed of her progress and of the pieces she was playing and inquired impatiently when her new harpsichord would come. She even kept on with her drawing; in one letter she told her father that she had done a landscape in which she included a little man playing the violin. Jefferson told her to listen for the song of the nightingales, which he loved, and compare it with that of the southern mocking birds.[15]

Polly (Maria) Jefferson reluctantly joined Patsy and her father in Paris in July 1787. Her usually solicitous father does not seem to have realized what a physical and emotional shock it was for the little girl to leave the Eppeses (see above, p. 19n), the only family she had ever known, be decoyed aboard a ship, and make the long journey to Europe accompanied only by a young black girl. They came by way of the Adamses in London. Abby Adams described how upset the little girl was—"in affliction" at meeting so many strangers. She was further frightened by the fact that her father could not get away from his work to come to get her, but sent his steward Petit instead. Abby

[11] TJ, Annapolis, to Martha Jefferson, Philadelphia, Nov. 28, 1783, Boyd VI, 360.

[12] Account Books, Nov. 17, 18, 19, 21, 1783.

[13] Hastings, pp. 334–35. Du Simitière was a well-known artist. He designed the great seals for the states of Georgia, Delaware, and Virginia, and submitted a design for the Great Seal of the United States. *Ibid.*, pp. 217, 254.

[14] Loesser, p. 317.

[15] Martha Jefferson, Paris, to TJ, Aix-en-Provence, [Mar. 8] and Apr. 9, 1787, Boyd XI, 203, 283; TJ to Martha, May 21, 1787, *ibid.*, 370.

hated to see her "doomed" to be shut up in a convent.[16] Polly, however, adjusted pretty well to her new life. Her father kept her former guardian, Mrs. Francis Eppes, up to date on her progress with French, Spanish, the harpsichord, and drawing.[17] When Jefferson withdrew the girls from Panthémont he continued to pay Balbastre 144 livres per month to give them harpsichord lessons. Polly also had guitar lessons; Jefferson had bought her an instrument and paid 36 livres per month for her lessons.[18]

Patsy married Thomas Mann Randolph, Jr., who was anything but a blockhead, in February 1790, shortly after the Jeffersons came home from Paris. Polly spent some time with her father, but was not always able to keep up with him; during the 1790s he was frequently in New York and Philadelphia, as Secretary of State and later as Vice-President of the United States. While Polly was with him in Philadelphia she had music lessons from John Christopher Moller, the best available teacher (see Chapter II).[19] Polly spent the rest of her time with her sister or with her Eppes cousins. Her father, in his letters, told her how much he missed his family and how sorry he was that they had "such a vagrant for a father," and always asked her how her music and other studies were progressing. On a trip to Richmond she let her music lapse, but she kept at it sufficiently to ask him to buy new jacks for the pianoforte (she meant the spinet; see Chapter IV) at Monticello and to take singing lessons with her Eppes cousins. When Polly was in Philadelphia, her father asked her new brother-in-law, Thomas Mann Randolph, to forward her books and music and told them that she and Nelly Custis often practiced together.[20]

Patsy Randolph, pregnant and running the household at Monticello early in 1791, worried about what her father would think of her temporary lapse in reading and music. She was also trying to supervise Polly's studies. She put her own Kirkman harpsichord in order,

[16] Roof, pp. 152–53.

[17] TJ, Paris, to Mrs. Elizabeth W. Eppes, Eppington, July 12, 1788, Boyd XIII, 347. Mrs. Eppes was the sister of Polly's mother. Polly later married Mrs. Eppes's son (her cousin), John Wayles Eppes.

[18] Account Books, Sept. 5, 1788; Apr. 6, May 2, 15, 30, June 1, 26, July 2, Aug. 1, 2, Sept. 3, 5, 24, Oct. 4, 1789.

[19] *Ibid.*, Oct. 31, Nov. 8, 15, 1792; Apr. 14, May 6, 1793.

[20] TJ, New York, to Maria Jefferson, Apr. 11, 1790, and Maria, Richmond, to TJ, Apr. 25, 1790, Betts and Bear, pp. 52–53. Maria Jefferson, Eppington, to TJ, July 20 and Aug. 11, 1790, Boyd XVII, 239, 333. TJ, Philadelphia, to Thomas Mann Randolph, Monticello, Nov. 24, 1791; Maria Jefferson, Philadelphia, to Thomas Mann Randolph, Dec. 25, 1791; TJ, Philadelphia, to Thomas Mann Randolph, Monticello, Feb. 20, 1792, TJ Papers, DLC. TJ, Germantown, to Maria Jefferson, Nov. 17, 1793, TJ Papers, MHi.

but Polly did not show any great desire to use it. Polly was, according to her sister, "remarkably docile where she can surmount her Laziness of which she has an astonishing degree and which makes her neglect whatever she thinks will not be immediately discovered."[21] After Patsy had her baby (Anne Cary Randolph, her first) the new grandfather teasingly asked Polly if she had begun giving her new niece harpsichord and Spanish lessons yet.[22] Polly's chronic laziness was probably due to general ill-health and frailty, augmented by her feeling that she could never equal Patsy in either intellectual attainment or in her father's affections. She later found her greatest happiness with her husband, John Wayles Eppes.[23]

Both daughters spent part of the winter of 1802–3 in Washington with their father, the President of the United States. Both of their husbands were there serving in Congress. A contemporary described the two young ladies as "well-accomplished women, very delicate and tolerably handsome."[24] Mrs. Samuel Harrison Smith, wife of the publisher of the *National Intelligencer*, said that Maria Eppes was beautiful, timid in a group of people but good company alone. Martha Randolph was homely, she said, then softened this by adding that Martha was a "delicate likeness of her father," more interesting than Mrs. Eppes, and one of the "most lovely" women ever. Mrs. Smith was enchanted with Martha's daughter Ellen and called her "one of the finest and most intelligent children I have ever met with."[25]

Mr. Jefferson spent his retirement years surrounded by his grandchildren, the children of Martha Randolph, most of whom were girls. Martha attempted to give her girls the same kind of education she had had, with her father supervising and guiding their studies as he had hers. Martha had the formidable task of educating the girls with no outside help. She never sent them away from home to school, and

[21] Martha Jefferson Randolph, Monticello, to TJ, Jan. 16, 1791, Betts and Bear *Family Letters*, p. 68.

[22] TJ, Philadelphia, to Maria Jefferson, Monticello, Feb. 16, 1791, *ibid.*, p. 72.

[23] Many years later, Henry Stephens Randall, in the third volume of his biography of Jefferson, used some family letters in his text to describe various family members. He apparently toned down a letter in which Ellen Randolph Coolidge, Patsy's daughter, commented on the differences between her mother and her Aunt Maria. Ellen did not like his abridgement: she wrote, "Again the published letter speaking of my own mother says, 'She was intellectually somewhat superior to her sister.' The word *somewhat* is Mr. Randall's own; I never could have used it for my mother was intellectually *very greatly* superior to her sister." Manuscript notebook, p. 41, EWC, ViU.

[24] Anne H. Wharton, *Social Life in the Early Republic* (Philadelphia, 1902), p. 110.

[25] Hunt, pp. 33–34.

she certainly would never find music teachers of the quality of Bentley, Moller, and Balbastre in Albemarle County. Nevertheless, Martha and her father educated the girls far beyond the scope of the average Virginia girl's learning. At times Martha was discouraged about the children's progress—"surely if they turn out well with regard to morals I *ought* to be satisfied," she wrote to her father, "tho I *feel* that I never can sit down quietly under the idea of their being blockheads."[26] They were definitely not blockheads. Martha's husband, who had little to do with the children, nevertheless paid tribute to her work: "The good temper and promising qualities of the children, their steady health, fine growth and progress in their education which she [Martha] directs and labors with all her powers make her feel and declare herself frequently to be as happy as any person on earth."[27] No doubt her greatest happiness came from the fact that her father was pleased with her efforts. Her daughter Ellen passed along his opinion: "Grandpapa and myself are in the habit of sitting, sometime after dinner, in conversation, upon different subjects, and it was but the other day, that, speaking of education, and the influence exerted by mothers over their children, he paid to his grandchildren the compliment of all others the most valuable, that of alluding indirectly to what he considers their excellences, and ascribing them to education and example."[28]

The older Randolph girls, Anne Cary, Ellen, Cornelia, and Virginia were the closest to their grandfather and were his "little playmates." Anne Cary, the oldest, was first to marry and leave Monticello. Ellen and Virginia were the favorites, and left many written comments about their very special relationship with Jefferson. He gave Ellen, among other things, her first watch and a beautiful saddle. He gave Virginia an expensive guitar and her first silk dress. "My Bible came from him," wrote Ellen, "my Shakspeare, my first writing-table, my first handsome writing-desk, my first Leghorn hat, my first silk dress. . . . Our grandfather seemed to read our hearts, to see our invisible wishes, to be our good genius, to wave the fairy wand, to brighten our young lives by his goodness and his gifts."[29]

[26] Martha Jefferson Randolph, Edgehill, to TJ, Washington, Apr. 16, 1802, Betts and Bear, *Family Letters*, p. 223.

[27] Thomas Mann Randolph, Edgehill, to TJ, Washington, Feb. 6, 1802, EHR, ViU.

[28] [Ellen Wayles Randolph], Poplar Forest, to [Martha Jefferson Randolph], Monticello, July 28, 1819, EWC, ViU.

[29] Letter to Henry Stephens Randall from Ellen Wayles Randolph Coolidge, ca. 1850, quoted in Randolph, *Domestic Life*, pp. 295–96. Grandfather's "fairy wand" was money that came from unpaid labor or from his long-suffering creditors.

The girls, Ellen especially, were also great favorites with other people. One of the many visitors to Monticello tells us that Ellen was "the best talker I have ever heard among women . . . not beautiful but is genteel and good-looking enough."[30] Another opinion of the girls at Monticello comes from Peggy Nicholas, mother of Thomas Jefferson (Jeff) Randolph's wife Jane. Mrs. Nicholas thought that the Randolph girls were stiff and ill at ease in company as a result of having spent too much time at Monticello and not having socialized much with their Albemarle neighbors. Ellen and Cornelia were the "most stylish, elegant looking girls that I meet with in any company. Ellen, when her face is lighted up in conversation, is certainly the most beautiful, too, that I have met with. Cornelia has a fine figure and would be an elegant girl if she could be a little more at her ease. . . . Ellen would be greatly admired if she had not such a tell-tale countenance. She shows too plainly that she feels her superiority."[31]

Jefferson kept his girls busy with the harpsichord, Greek and Roman history, French, astronomy, and other pursuits. He also expected each of them to take a month's turn at running the entire Monticello household. Virginia's letters to her fiancé, Nicholas Trist, reveal that she took her turn at housekeeping, cooking, sewing, serving as Jefferson's secretary, practicing the harpsichord and keeping up with her studies. There were always so many people around, both family and visitors, that she had no privacy. She finally found a small unused room over the parlor portico, moved a few things into it and claimed it as her own.[32]

Virginia and Ellen were the musicians. Both played the harpsichord, Ellen with considerably more alacrity than Virginia, who also played the guitar and sang. And the girls really did socialize more than Peggy Nicholas would have us believe, and they mixed in far more cosmopolitan company than Albemarle County society. They traveled around Virginia to visit various cousins, and they went to Washington and Philadelphia with relatives and friends. They took turns going to Richmond with their father when he was governor of Virginia. Ellen wrote many lively letters home, giving her mother

[30] Monticello Archives, Monticello. Quoted from a letter of Dr. Horace Holley to his brother, Sept. 6, 1824.

[31] Peggy Nicholas [Mrs. Wilson Cary Nicholas] to Jane Hollins Nicholas Randolph [Mrs. Thomas Jefferson Randolph], Jan. 8, 1818, EHR, ViU.

[32] Barbara Mayo, "Twilight at Monticello," *Virginia Quarterly Review* 17 (1941): 509–10. Nicholas Philip Trist and his brother Hore Browse Trist were the grandsons of Mrs. Elizabeth Trist, a long-time friend of Jefferson. Nicholas Trist is known to historians as the man who negotiated the Treaty of Guadalupe-Hidalgo with Mexico in 1848.

and grandfather her impressions of whomever and whatever she saw. She always searched out new music, both printed and in manuscript. She was usually lucky enough to stay where she had a piano to practice on. Her letters sound as if she missed her music very much indeed when a piano was not available. She particularly missed her music when she went to Poplar Forest with Jefferson.[33]

Ellen shared with her family the music to which she was exposed. In Washington she heard a harpist whom she considered excellent as a harpist but impossible as a singer: "his voice is so bad as to destroy the effect of his harp."[34] She ran across a volume of Thomas Moore's poems, *Irish Melodies*, and because she thought they were beautiful and she knew the family liked them, she intended to copy some and send them home.[35] A few years later, in Richmond, she heard a young bank cashier from Philadelphia sing and thought he was so good that "if he were not evidently a well bred man, acquainted in the best of Philadelphia circles, I should suspect that music had been taught him as a profession."[36] The young man was not only a good singer, he was very attentive to Ellen. She was so moved by his singing that she threatened to "tear my music books, break my piano (if I had one) and sit down in calm desperation at the utter impossibility of ever tolerating any music that I am likely to hear again."[37] Unfortunately the young man was not very sincere, for he apparently organized a social event so that he could sing again for Ellen and, when asked to sing, said that he did not feel like it and walked out.[38]

Since Ellen's tastes in music had been formed by her mother and grandfather, she did not greatly care for the waltzes fashionable in the early nineteenth century. She thought that she might collect some of them but soon tired of them: "that insipid family of Waltzes, all so much alike, and striving to make up in difficulty of execution what

[33] [Ellen Wayles Randolph], Poplar Forest, to [Martha Jefferson Randolph], Monticello, Aug. 24, 1819, and [Ellen] to Virginia Jefferson Randolph, Monticello, Jan. 9, 1820, EWC, ViU. Poplar Forest was a property of Jefferson's in Bedford County that he used as a retreat when he wanted to escape the constant stream of visitors to Monticello.

[34] [Ellen Wayles Randolph], Washington, to [Martha Jefferson Randolph], Feb. 17, 1816, EWC, ViU.

[35] [Ellen Wayles Randolph], Washington, to Virginia Jefferson Randolph, Monticello, Feb. 28, 1816, EWC, ViU.

[36] [Ellen Wayles Randolph], Richmond, to Martha Jefferson Randolph, Monticello, May 18, 1820, EWC, ViU.

[37] *Ibid.*

[38] [Ellen Wayles Randolph], Richmond, to [Martha Jefferson Randolph], May 31, 1820, EWC, ViU.

they want in genius, has already exhausted my patience and I am heartily sick of them all. It would require a quire of paper to enumerate the names of these tiresome things, with their never ending variations. We have, the Danish, the Swiss, the Bohemian, the Munich, the Stantz, the Stamitz, the Russian, the Memel, the Hanoverian, Pampelunian, Brazilian, &c, &c, &c, &c."[39]

Virginia was not as eager about practice or as sure of her talents as Ellen. Family letters give the impression that everybody constantly nagged at her to practice. Ellen once suggested to her a piece that was "not difficult" but would "*require practice*."[40] Nicholas Trist commanded her to practice as often as possible.[41] Her mother hoped that she kept up with her music on one of her Richmond visits and asked her to copy some music and send it home.[42] Later her mother wrote to Nicholas and told him that since returning from Richmond, Virginia had enthusiastically taken up her harpsichord practice again. Virginia's story was different; she despaired of ever acquiring the right touch, and although she was trying very hard to learn some of Nicholas's favorite tunes, she said that he couldn't possibly hate reading law as much as she hated the harpsichord. Even Jefferson scolded her about neglecting the harpsichord, but to little avail.[43] Virginia was much more cheerful about practicing on the guitars that Jefferson and her cousin gave her (see Chapter IV). She had guitar instruction books that friends and family sent her. She practiced the guitar regularly, and enjoyed singing to her own accompaniment.[44]

Virginia ultimately outgrew her aversion for the harpsichord and became so proficient a keyboard performer that Jefferson, her mother, and Nicholas wanted her to have a new piano. The four of them overwhelmed all opposition to the purchase (see Chapter IV)

[39] See above, n. 36.

[40] [Ellen Wayles Randolph], Poplar Forest, to [Martha Jefferson Randolph], Monticello, Aug. 18, 1817, EWC, ViU.

[41] Nicholas Trist, Lafourche, Louisiana, to Virginia Jefferson Randolph, Monticello, Jan. 1, 1822, NPT, NcU.

[42] Martha Jefferson Randolph, Monticello, to Virginia Jefferson Randolph, Richmond, Jan. 27, 1822, NPT, NcU.

[43] Martha Jefferson Randolph, Monticello, to Nicholas Trist, Lafourche, Louisiana, Mar. 21, 1822, NPT, NcU. Virginia Jefferson Randolph, Monticello, to Nicholas Trist, Lafourche, Louisiana, Mar. 15 and Apr. 28, 1822, and Dec. 12, 1823, NPT, DLC.

[44] [Ellen Wayles Randolph], Washington, to [Martha Jefferson Randolph], Monticello, Mar. [?], 1816, EWC, ViU. Virginia Jefferson Randolph, Monticello, to Nicholas Trist, Lafourche, Louisiana, Feb. 6 and Mar. 21, 1824, NPT, DLC.

and asked Ellen and her husband to get them a piano in Boston. Virginia talked about what an enjoyment the piano would be for Jefferson, her mother, Nicholas, and herself, and how "music is really the only thing I have a natural and decided taste for."[45] She felt that her brother Jeff (Thomas Jefferson Randolph), in objecting to the purchase, did not "take at all into consideration the time I have spent practicing on an old instrument too far gone even to learn on."[46] Virginia promised everyone that she would practice regularly and faithfully when the piano came, and she seems to have done so.[47]

Ellen left Monticello when she married Joseph Coolidge, Jr., of Boston in 1825. Grandpapa approved her choice but missed her dreadfully: "I fear he misses you sadly every evening when he takes his seat in one of the Campeachy chairs, and he looks so solitary and the empty chair on the opposite side of the door is such a melancholy sight to us all, that one or the other of us is sure to go and occupy it, though we can not possibly fill the vacancy you have left in his society."[48] The family sent Ellen her trunks, containing her personal possessions and her music. Unfortunately the ship carrying them sank. Her mother and the girls assured Ellen that they would copy anything she wanted from their own large collection. She was to send them music paper with Virginia's new piano.[49]

Ellen had a new Broadwood grand piano. It was not then well broken in, and its action was very stiff. Ellen wished her mother could be with her in Boston to help make the piano's action supple. Virginia told Ellen that her mother said not to worry about the stiffness of the new piano: "her harpsichord for some time after she got it was so stiff that she might have played with nearly as much ease on a brick pavement." One of their brother Jeff's little girls made up a

[45] Virginia Randolph Trist, Monticello, to Ellen Wayles Coolidge, Boston, Sept. 3, 1825, EWC, ViU.

[46] *Ibid.* Ellen usually wrote little abstracts on the backs of letters she received. On this one she wrote: "Virginia's great fault is a disposition to *depreciate* herself—to undercolor her own good qualities and exaggerate her defects. For her friends, on the contrary, she just reverses the process—amplifying their virtues and excusing their short comings." This is also the letter that contains all of the information about the family row over Virginia's new piano (see Chapter IV).

[47] Virginia Randolph Trist, Monticello, to Ellen Wayles Coolidge, Boston, Dec. 4, 1825, EWC, ViU.

[48] [Virginia Randolph Trist], Monticello, to Ellen Wayles Coolidge, New York, June 27, 1825, EWC, ViU.

[49] Martha Jefferson Randolph, Monticello, to Ellen Wayles Coolidge, Boston, Oct. 13, 1825; Mary Jefferson Randolph, Monticello, to Ellen Wayles Coolidge, Boston, Nov. 10, 1825; Mrs. Randolph to Ellen, Nov. 16, 1825; Ellen to Mrs. Randolph, Nov. 20, 1825, EWC, ViU.

story about how all of the children were going to go to Boston to see Aunt Coolidge, "who will be playing the piano when they arrive."[50]

The girls' musical life at Monticello was not all dreary practice to try to attain the high standards set by their mother and grandfather. There were always several young men around, usually cousins Francis Eppes (Maria's son) and Wayles Baker, and the Trist brothers, Nicholas and Hore Browse. They often sang and danced in the evenings, either to the music of a Negro fiddler or to the old harpsichord. They never mention Jefferson's playing for them, although he and their mother encouraged their activity and enjoyed watching the dancing. Several of the girls and boys played flageolets. Cornelia Randolph had one and so did both of the Trist boys. Browse Trist gave his to Lewis Randolph, the younger brother who also got Jefferson's small violin.[51]

Of the younger Randolph children, only Septimia was musical, and she was too young for Jefferson to direct her education as he had the older girls. The only thing he could do to promote the musical education of the younger children was to see that they learned to dance. He paid a local dancing teacher, Xaupi, about sixty dollars for lessons for Ben, Mary, Lewis, and Septimia.[52] Lewis must have been musical to at least a certain degree if Jefferson gave him a violin, but there is no record of his ever taking music lessons.

After her father's death Martha Randolph continued to teach music to her youngest daughter Septimia and to her grandchildren. For part of the time that she lived at Edgehill with Jeff Randolph's family, she had six music students—four of Jeff's daughters and two neighbors. Throughout her father's life she had nearly always played for him in the evening after tea; to the end of her own life she continued to play his favorite songs.[53]

[50] Virginia Randolph Trist, Monticello, to Ellen Wayles Coolidge, Boston, Oct. 16, 1825, and Ellen to Mrs. Randolph, Jan. 2, 1826, EWC, ViU. John Broadwood and Sons, London, was a world-famous firm making keyboard instruments. The firm was founded in 1728 by Burkat Shudi, harpsichord maker. The first John Broadwood joined the firm in 1769, having worked for Shudi for several years. For many years the firm was known as Shudi and Broadwood. After 1782, however, Broadwood was the sole proprietor.

[51] Hore Browse Trist, Monticello, to Nicholas Trist, West Point, Jan. 1, May 13, June 27, 1819; Mrs. Elizabeth Trist [the Trist boys' grandmother, and a long-time friend of TJ], Farmington, to Nicholas Trist, West Point, June 27, 1819, NPT, DLC. Cornelia Jefferson Randolph, Ashton, to Virginia Jefferson Randolph, Poplar Forest, Dec. 1, 1820; Nicholas Trist, Lafourche, Louisiana, to Virginia Jefferson Randolph, Monticello, Sept. 13, 1823, NPT, NcU.

[52] Account Books, July 9 and Aug. 26, 1824; May 13, 1825.

[53] Randolph, "Mrs. Thomas Mann Randolph," p. 46.

CHAPTER IV

Thomas Jefferson's Musical Instruments

A VERITABLE PROCESSION of fine musical instruments, especially keyboard instruments, followed each other into and out of Jefferson's various places of residence. He never shopped for instruments, comparing varieties and prices; he simply decided what he wanted and ordered it, often describing in detail exactly how he wanted the instrument constructed inside and out and what accessories and parts he thought he would need in order to keep it in good repair, which he did. Frequent entries in the account books record costs of repairs and tunings. His correspondence shows that he knew how to tune his keyboard instruments and usually did so once the instruments came to Monticello. He did extensive restoration on a harpsichord and put it back in playing condition at a time when most people were no longer interested in harpsichords. He was always interested in new developments or inventions that might improve certain musical instruments. It is virtually impossible to determine exactly how many instruments he had. We know that he bought a Kirkman harpsichord for each of his daughters, but the account books and family correspondence contain too many duplications, repetitions, and obscurities to permit tabulation of his other keyboard instruments, violins, guitars, and musical gadgets. Nevertheless, it is interesting to piece together a history of what can be discovered about Jefferson's musical instruments and what finally happened to them.

No description of Jefferson's instruments would be complete without mentioning several items that interested him enough to cause him to inquire about them, but which he did not buy. These include a clavichord, an organ, a glass harmonica, and a piano. Late in 1770 or early in 1771, he instructed Thomas Adams of London to purchase a number of things for him, but particularly a clavichord, a gift for his future wife, Martha Wayles Skelton. He asked that Adams get the clavichord as quickly as possible and purchase it in Hamburg because he thought Hamburg clavichords were the best and the cheapest. He lost interest in the clavichord as soon as he saw a piano, however, and changed his order.[1]

[1] TJ, Monticello, to Thomas Adams, London, Feb. 20 and June 1, 1771, Boyd I, 62, 71–72.

On two occasions he seriously considered buying an organ. Robert Carter of Nomini Hall and Williamsburg had a fine one in his Williamsburg house. He had had it built in London to his own specifications. Jefferson offered to buy it, but Carter did not want to sell. He told Jefferson that his daughters played it; their music teacher had entered the Continental army, but had recently resigned and the Carters were expecting him to teach their girls upon his return.[2] Several years later, during his residence in France, Jefferson wrote to Dr .Charles Burney asking for more information on organs. Did the English or the French make the best organs? He knew that London craftsmen built the best harpsichords and pianos, but he did not visit a London organ builder on his brief trip to England. Who was the best London craftsman, and what would be the right kind of organ for a room twenty-four feet square and eighteen feet high? Burney assured him that English organs were far superior to French ones, informing him that Green of London was the best builder, and that an organ of the kind he wanted would cost about a hundred pounds.[3]

The glass harmonica was another instrument that fascinated Jefferson enough for him to think about buying one. He wanted one of six-octave compass, in a plain mahogany case. His friend John Trumbull told him that three octaves was the limit on glass harmonicas and that he could buy one from Longman and Broderip of London for thirty guineas.[4] However, Jefferson never bought one.

Jefferson once refused a piano, giving lack of funds as his excuse. He had sent Thomas Claxton, the official decorator for the President's House, to Philadelphia to buy a number of things. Claxton thought that a fortepiano might be "pleasing to everyone" and suggested that Jefferson authorize him to have a "skillful person" select one. Jefferson replied that "no doubt a Pianoforte would be a perfectly proper piece of furniture. But in the present state of our funds, they will be exhausted by articles more indispensable." He went on to say that he did not want to buy a piano until he saw whether or not John Isaac Hawkins's experiments with pianos were going to be successful.[5]

[2] Robert Carter to TJ, June 27, 1778, Boyd II, 206; Morton, p. 219. Carter eventually sold the organ to a relative of George Washington. Molnar, "Art Music in Colonial Virginia," p. 74, n. 137.

[3] TJ, Paris, to Charles Burney, London, July 10, 1786, Boyd IX, 118; Burney to TJ, Jan. 20, 1787, Boyd XI, 59.

[4] TJ, Paris, to John Trumbull, London, Oct. 11, 1787, and Trumbull to TJ, Oct. 30, 1787, Boyd XII, 235, 297.

[5] Boyd XV, xxxi; Thomas Claxton, Philadelphia, to TJ, Washington, June 13, 1802, and TJ to Claxton, June 18, 1802, MHi. For more about Hawkins's experiments, see below, pp. 55–57, 74–75.

Jefferson rented keyboard instruments for his daughter Patsy to practice on whenever he happened to be temporarily without an instrument of his own. He rented a clavichord and its stand for Patsy while they were in Philadelphia waiting to leave for Europe.[6] Later, in Paris, he paid twelve francs per month rental for a pianoforte for two years, until Patsy's new Kirkman harpsichord arrived from London.[7]

Jefferson probably bought his first piano sometime in 1771 as a present for his wife, changing his original order from a clavichord to a piano because he had seen one of the new fortepianos and was "charmed with it." Although he described what he wanted he did not specify a craftsman from whom to get it. There would have been no problem; Adams, his agent, was in London and London was the center of piano-building at that time. On April 29, 1779, Jefferson noted in his account book that he "sold my piano forte to Gen. Riedesel, he is to give me £100."[8] He gave no reason for the sale, nor is there any record of Riedesel's actually having paid for the piano. Neither Riedesel nor his wife mention this transaction in the diaries of their stay in Virginia. A letter written by another German and printed in a Hamburg newspaper described the Jefferson household and said that there was at Monticello an "Elegant harpsichord piano-forte."[9] He was probably referring either to Martha's piano before Riedesel bought it or to her spinet. Since there is no other mention anywhere of Martha's piano, it is possible that Riedesel actually did buy it and take it back to Germany with him.

Considering that Thomas Jefferson was a violinist of some skill and much enthusiasm, it is surprising that he has left only the scantiest of references to his violins in his correspondence and his account books. He recorded only three violin purchases: in 1768 he bought a violin for five pounds from Dr. William Pasteur, a Williamsburg druggist, and twenty years later he bought a "small violin" in Paris for thirty-six livres. He paid thirteen pounds in 1775 for a third violin, which he got from John Randolph.[10]

This last acquisition was the result of a facetious bargain he made in 1771 with John Randolph of Williamsburg, attorney-general for

[6] Account Books, Nov. 17, 1783; Nov. 19, 1783; Nov. 21, 1783.

[7] *Ibid.*, Jan 8, Mar. 3, May 2, June 3, July 1, Aug. 3, Sept. 7, Oct. 10, Nov. 8, Dec. 10, 1785; Jan. 9, Feb. 10, May 6, June 9, July 10, Aug. 9, Sept. 13, Oct. 13, Nov. 6, Dec. 9, 1786; Feb. 13, 1787.

[8] *Ibid.*, April 29, 1779.

[9] Jacob Rubsamen to TJ, Dec. 1, 1780, Boyd IV, 174.

[10] Account Books, May 25, 1768; Aug. 17, 1775; Aug. 15, 1788.

the crown. Randolph had a violin that was supposed to be a good one, perhaps even a good Italian one, and Jefferson admired it. The two men made an agreement and recorded it, with seven witnesses, at the general court in Williamsburg. If Randolph survived Jefferson, he was to get his choice of books from Jefferson's library, to the value of a hundred pounds. If Jefferson survived Randolph, he was to get the violin and any music Randolph had for it, or sixty pounds' worth of Randolph's books. In 1775 Randolph, a Loyalist, decided to return to England. He asked Carter Braxton to tell Jefferson he would sell the violin. Jefferson sent a messenger for it, with a draft, and also requested the music. He thought that the violin had no case, therefore he wanted it carefully wrapped in cloth and packed in a wooden box. Randolph left the violin with a Mr. Cocke of Williamsburg. Jefferson duly noted in his account book that on August 17, 1775, he gave Carter Braxton a draft for thirteen pounds for the violin and that the purchase dissolved the bargain with Randolph and the legacy to him.[11]

We may reasonably believe that Jefferson must have had during his lifetime other violins than the ones specifically mentioned in his accounts. Even as a boy he must have had the use of a violin, since he had learned to play one before he entered James Maury's school. He surely had a violin of his own when he played duets with Patrick Henry during the Christmas holidays of 1759, and when he played at the Governor's Palace during his early Williamsburg days.[12] He told his grandson-in-law, Nicholas Trist, that he gave his kit to a grandson, Meriwether Lewis Randolph.[13] In 1770 the original Jefferson family home at Shadwell burned and Jefferson lost everything. According to family tradition, a slave saved his fiddle or one of them.[14] The lucky fiddle could have been either the Pasteur violin or one whose purchase went unrecorded.

Isaac, a slave at Monticello, said that his master kept three fiddles.[15] An unnamed former student at the University of Virginia told an interviewer that Jefferson had once given him a "portable fiddle." He described it as a "small narrow one he [Jefferson] had made in Paris in order to carry it about with him for practice," and added that its tones were "none of the best." The former student returned the

[11] Boyd I, 66–67, 240, 243, 244; Account Books, Aug. 17, 1775.

[12] TJ, Monticello, to William Wirt, Aug. 5, 1815, TJ Additionals, ViU; Parton, 25, 30; Malone I, 78–79.

[13] Trist, Memorandum. Kits were small violins usually used by dancing masters.

[14] Randolph, *Domestic Life*, p. 43.

[15] Isaac Jefferson, p. 13.

little fiddle to the estate after Jefferson's death, although Thomas Jefferson Randolph told him that he should have kept it.[16] Near the end of his life, Jefferson told Nicholas Trist he still had two fine violins that would fetch a high price in London—the Randolph violin and "a Cremona more than a hundred years old."[17] These two, plus the kit, could be the three to which Isaac referred, if Isaac really did know how many violins his master had.

Rumors persist that one of Jefferson's violins was not only a Cremona, but one of great value. The most likely candidate for this honor is the Pasteur violin. From advertisements and evaluations of estates, we know that alleged Cremona and Stainer violins were plentiful in Virginia by the middle of the eighteenth century. Good ones as well as good copies sold for from five to fifteen pounds.[18] At the time Jefferson bought the Pasteur and Randolph violins, Nicola Amati (1596–1684) of Cremona and Jacob Stainer (1621–1683) of Absam in the Tyrol were virtually the only individual violinmakers who were sufficiently well known for their violins to have escalated in price. A genuine Nicola Amati or Stainer would have cost at least four times as much as Jefferson paid for either the Pasteur or the Randolph violin. The prices he paid are more in line with late eighteenth-century prices of the violins of Stradivarius, the Guarneri family, the minor Amatis, or any one of a host of talented but unknown Italian and German violinmakers. The labels in violins mean nothing. Scores of violinmakers copied both the styles and labels of the better-known makers.[19]

All we know about the two violins that Jefferson kept until the end of his life comes from the letters of another grandson-in-law, Joseph Coolidge, Jr., of Boston. Coolidge believed that the violins were valuable, and tried to sell them advantageously after Jefferson's death. Coolidge included them on a list of Monticello articles that he wanted to purchase, and several times he inquired of Nicholas Trist whether or not the family was going to sell them, and if so, where?[20] He did

16 Frederick Daniel, "Virginian Reminiscences of Jefferson," *Harper's Weekly* 48 (1904): 1766, 1768.

17 Trist, Memorandum.

18 Stoutamire, pp. 16–17. See also advertisements and excerpts from estate inventories in: Helen Duprey Bullock, "On Music in Colonial Williamsburg"; and Mary Goodwin, "Musical Instruments in Eighteenth Century America," both MS. reports in the Research Department, The Colonial Williamsburg Foundation.

19 W. Henry and Alfred E. Hill, *Antonio Stradivari: His Life and Work* (New York, 1962), pp. 213, 246–50.

20 Joseph Coolidge, Jr., Memorandum of Aug. 30, 1826; Joseph Coolidge,

not want them put up for sale with the rest of the Monticello furnishings at Charlottesville, "where they don't know the difference between a Cremona and a $5 fiddle."[21] He asked Trist "if the Cremona with the maker's name pasted in it was made by Amati or Guarnerius, or Stradivarius?"[22] Coolidge eventually wrote of having received the violins, but he never again mentioned their labels. He had them examined by a "celebrated performer." Although the violins had no strings and their bridges were broken, the performer pronounced the Cremona admirable and thought that Coolidge should get 150 guineas for it in London. Coolidge sent the violins to London with a friend and eventually received word that they arrived safely. Disappointed in the sale of Jefferson's paintings, he hoped that the family would realize more from the instruments.[23]

Were the Randolph violin and the "Cremona" really valuable? Did they sell, or did they return ignominiously from England, their supposed pedigrees demolished by real experts? No one knows. There is one other tantalizing and incomplete clue. Twenty-five years after the violins went to England, Coolidge asked his brother-in-law, George Wythe Randolph, what happened to "Grandpapa's violin." George, in turn, asked one of Thomas Jefferson Randolph's daughters, specifying that he meant the one that was "supposed to be a Cremona."[24] This might indicate that at least one of the violins came home from England in disgrace and disappeared from sight in the throng of Randolph children, grandchildren, and cousins.

An enumeration of Jefferson's violins from available evidence shows that:

1. He had a kit.
2. Family tradition claims that a slave rescued a violin from the Shadwell fire.

Jr., Boston, to Nicholas Trist, Monticello, Jan. 5, Mar. 8, Dec. 4, 1827, NPT, DLC.

[21] Coolidge to Trist, Oct. 25, 1826, NPT, DLC.

[22] Coolidge to Trist, Mar. 24, 1828, NPT, DLC. By this time, dealers and musicians recognized the excellence of these three violinmakers. Other violinmakers recognized it too, and inundated the market with copies containing the labels of these three.

[23] Ellen Wayles Coolidge, Boston, to Martha Jefferson Randolph, Baltimore (forwarded to Richmond), May 6, 1828; Joseph Coolidge, Jr., Boston, to Martha Jefferson Randolph, Monticello, Aug. 7, 1828; Coolidge to Mrs. Randolph, Edgehill, Jan. 12, 1829; EWC, ViU. Coolidge, Boston, to Trist, Monticello, [?] May, July 9, Oct. 7, 1828; NPT, DLC. Coolidge's "celebrated performer" was not necessarily an expert at evaluating violins.

[24] George Wythe Randolph to Mary Buchanan Randolph, Mar. 18 and Mar. 29, 1855, EHR, ViU.

3. He bought two violins, one from Pasteur and one in Paris.
4. He got a violin from John Randolph.
5. The slave Isaac said that he had three violins at Monticello ca. 1781–1824.
6. He gave the kit to his grandson Lewis and perhaps gave the Paris violin to a university student.
7. He had a "Cremona" and the Randolph violin until the end of his life.
8. Coolidge tried to sell these last two in England after Jefferson's death.

This still does not tell exactly how many violins Jefferson owned, but gives evidence that he could have owned at least five—the kit, the Pasteur purchase, the Paris purchase, the "Cremona," and the Randolph. This does not account for violins he may have had as a child or others whose purchases went unrecorded. Since there is no record of the "Cremona's" purchase, it could very well have been the Pasteur instrument, especially if, as seems likely, the "Cremona" was either the product of an ordinary Italian violinmaker or a respectable copy of a first-rate Cremona. The "Cremona," the Pasteur, and the Shadwell violins could also be the same instrument, the slave having saved it for its known value as well as his master's love of it. One could speculate endlessly on how many violins there were, which was which, and what happened to them. It is not at all surprising that, over the years, so many "Jefferson violins" have emerged from various places with strange and interesting stories (see Appendix III).

The Monticello family owned at least two guitars and perhaps more. There were several guitarists in the family circle: Mrs. Jefferson, Maria, and three granddaughters, Virginia, Cornelia, and Septimia Randolph. The purchase of guitar strings from a Philadelphia merchant in 1776 indicates that there was a guitar in the house at that time.[25] In Paris, Jefferson paid eighty-four livres for a guitar for Maria (then called Polly) and shipped it home in the box numbered fourteen on his baggage list.[26] According to Virginia Randolph Trist, her grandfather bought her a beautiful Spanish or English guitar when she was about fifteen. It belonged to a neighbor who was moving out of the area and wanted to sell it. Virginia wanted it very badly, but knew that her family could not afford it. Jefferson bought it for her on the condition that she learn to play it. It was probably the thirty-dollar guitar purchase recorded in 1816.[27] Several years later Virginia received another guitar, perhaps the one bought for her

[25] Account Books, Aug. 31, 1776.

[26] *Ibid.*, Sept. 5, 1788; Boyd XV, 375.

[27] Barbara Mayo, 505; Randolph, *Domestic Life*, p. 348; Account Books, Mar. 4, 1816.

Aunt Maria in Paris. Virginia's father, Thomas Mann Randolph, brought it to her from Richmond. A cousin, Wayles Baker, had given it to Randolph. Baker said that Virginia's Aunt Maria Eppes had once given it to his mother, who in turn gave it to him.[28] Many years later, while living in France, Virginia still had a guitar; perhaps she kept one of these two and her sister Septimia took the other one.[29] Family tradition says that the little ten-string guitar presently at Monticello is one of the two that formerly belonged to Virginia Randolph Trist. One of Virginia's descendants gave it to the Monticello foundation.[30]

A "spinnet made mostly in the shape of a harpsichord"[31] flits elusively in and out among Jefferson's other instruments. There is no entry of its purchase anywhere. It is possible that Martha Skelton Jefferson had it before her marriage and brought it with her to Monticello. In one of his ledgers, Jefferson notes that as part of the settlement of his father-in-law's estate he paid bills owing to a Mr. Allegre and a Mr. Victor "for 2 years teaching Mrs. Jefferson on the Spinnet."[32] Jefferson also mentioned the spinet in correspondence to his friend Francis Hopkinson. In August 1790 he told Hopkinson that he had a good spinet at Monticello that had been played so much that its jacks had "strayed away." He sent one of the surviving jacks to Hopkinson and asked him to try to find a craftsman in Philadelphia who could make a set of new ones. Jefferson said that the spinet was the only instrument at Monticello at that time,[33] which may mean that he sold his wife's piano and that Patsy's harpsichord had not yet arrived from Richmond, following shipment from France. Jefferson took the spinet to Philadelphia two years later for his younger daughter Maria to use. He paid a Godfrey Vebrell, or Webrell, to repair it several times.[34] He shipped it home again in 1793, correcting his steward's entry on the packing list from "un forte piano" to "the Spinet."[35] One of the many people who visited Monticello after the

[28] Virginia Jefferson Randolph, Monticello, to Nicholas Trist, Donaldsonville, Louisiana, Jan. 9, 1824, NPT, NcU.

[29] Virginia Randolph Trist, St. Servan, France, to Nicholas Trist, Havana, July 7, 1839, NPT, NcU.

[30] Monticello Archives, Monticello.

[31] Isaac Jefferson, p. 13.

[32] Miscellaneous Accounts 1764–79, July 13, 1772, CSmH.

[33] TJ, New York, to Francis Hopkinson, Philadelphia, June 13, 1790, Boyd XVI, 490; TJ to Hopkinson, Aug. 14, 1790, Boyd XVII, 390.

[34] Account Books, Mar. 28, 1792; May 19, 1793.

[35] Packing list [1785], McGregor-Jefferson Papers, ViU. I have given this item the date 1793 because it fits perfectly the description of a furniture list

family sold the property said that she saw the old broken spinet in the garrett: "it was the first I ever saw, it has keys something like a piano, but it is much lower, and the frame not so large, and the shape of a harpsichord."[36] The instrument she was describing sounds more like a spinet than anything else. It was the right shape, it was too small to be a harpsichord, and in addition the lady would have recognized a harpsichord.

Jefferson bought two magnificent Kirkman harpsichords, one for each daughter. He bought the first in 1786 for his older daughter Martha (usually called Patsy).[37] Jefferson, in France, first contacted his friend John Paradise in London on May 25, 1786, asking him to order the harpsichord from Kirkman of London and to have Dr. Charles Burney supervise the building of it. He wanted the very best, as usual—a two-manual model, solid mahogany case with no inlay, and a Venetian swell. He very sensibly asked for simple stops so that he could maintain it himself, then not so sensibly ordered one of Adam Walker's celestine attachments, or celestinas, for it. Burney was delighted that Jefferson asked him to accept this commission. He sent Jefferson information on what he would be getting: the harpsichord's sides would be oak veneered with mahogany, to ensure stability in any climate. The price would be sixty-six guineas plus two and a half guineas for the leather cover and packing case. The music desk was free. Kirkman hated Walker's celestine attachment because he thought that the resin used with it was detrimental to the instrument and ruined its tone. Burney promised Jefferson that he would check thoroughly with Walker about the celestine attachment before going ahead and having it installed on the harpsichord.

Jefferson began to make the necessary arrangements to bring Patsy's new harpsichord to France. He asked Colonel William Stephens Smith, secretary of the American legation in London and son-in-law of John Adams, to take charge of paying for it and arranging

---

which TJ enclosed in a letter to Martha Jefferson Randolph. He shipped the items on the list home to Monticello from Philadelphia in 1793. See TJ, Philadelphia, to Martha Jefferson Randolph, Monticello, May 12, 1793, Betts and Bear, pp. 116–17.

[36] Mrs. Anne Royall, *Mrs. Royall's Southern Tour, or Second Series of the Black Book* (Washington, 1830), I, 90.

[37] The following references give the complete documentation for Patsy's Kirkman harpsichord: Account Books, Nov. 14, 22, 28, 1787; Dec. 1, 8, 1787; Mar. 1, 1788; Apr. 24, 1788; June 3, 1788; Nov. 6, 1788; Dec. 8, 1788; May 15, 1789. Boyd IX, 579; X, 75–76, 118, 175, 211, 417, 467, 507–8, 516; XI, 59, 90, 140–41, 168, 203, 282, 349, 370, 381, 395, 531, 598, 599; XII, 7, 47–49, 112, 138, 206–7, 323, 327, 337, 366, 367, 374, 505, 597; XIII, 145, 200; XV, 375; XVI, 81, 90.

for its transportation from Kirkman's shop to either Limozin at Havre or the Garveys at Rouen, for shipment to Paris. He asked Charles Gravier, Compte de Vergennes, the French minister of foreign affairs, for permission to import it from London, along with "harness for 3 horses" and "Two copying-presses, with paper and appendages." Vergennes "fixed" things so that Jefferson could bring the harpsichord to France on a diplomatic passport, but explained that normally a harpsichord, considered a luxury item, was not eligible for inclusion on the passport with the other articles. Smith assured Jefferson that his London credit was good and that Burney would try the harpsichord as soon as he came back from the country.

Eventually on January 20, 1787, Burney wrote and apologized for delaying so long in keeping Jefferson posted on the progress of the harpsichord. The harpsichord was now at Walker's. Burney praised the instrument highly; he had never heard one with a better tone or tried one with a better touch, and he had never seen a celestine attachment that worked as well as this one. Late in January, Smith wrote again to tell Jefferson that the harpsichord was finished. Jefferson wrote to both Burney and Smith immediately to tell them not to send the harpsichord until April; he would be away for two or three months, and after April the instrument was less likely to be injured by bad weather. For some reason he neglected to tell Patsy that he had delayed the shipment of her harpsichord. She was awaiting it with all of the enthusiasm of which a young girl is capable when expecting a very special expensive gift, and asked him in several letters why it did not arrive. He assumed that his London connections had shipped it when he had asked and told her to review all of her old music, and to learn some slow, simple melodies for the celestina.

He assumed wrongly. There was still no harpsichord when he returned to Paris. He sent his steward Adrien Petit to London, instructing him to find out what had happened. Either Mrs. Smith or her mother, Mrs. John Adams, would know. Petit was also to go to Kirkman's shop to find out whether or not the harpsichord was finished, when it would be ready to ship, and to make arrangements to ship it to the Garveys at Rouen. He wrote in July to the artist, John Trumbull, with instructions to have Kirkman pack it in woolen blankets inside its box, to protect it from dampness. There was still confusion. Trumbull paid Walker thirteen guineas for the celestina and paid Kirkman for putting the harpsichord aboard ship for Rouen, thinking that it was on the ship by the middle of August. Abigail Adams, however, wrote that early in September it was still at Kirkman's. Kirkman insisted that he had received no instructions concerning what to do with it, only those directions to write and say

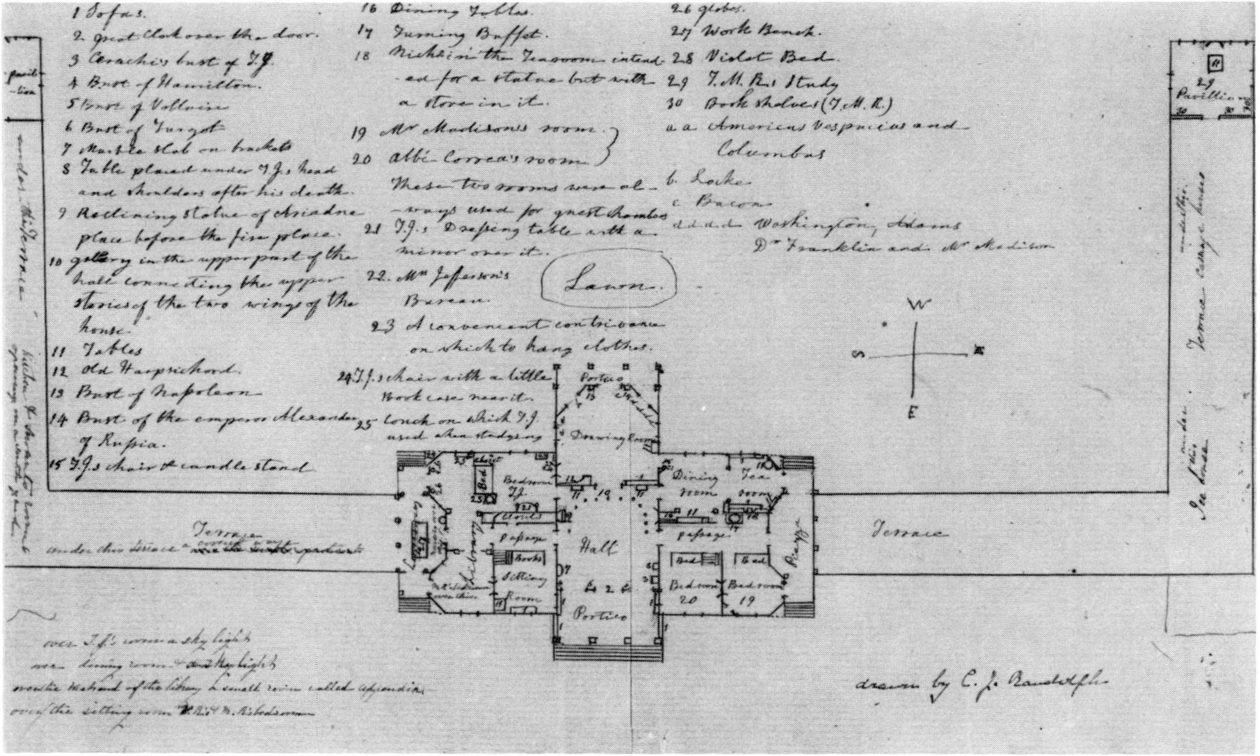

1 Cornelia Jefferson Randolph's drawing of the ground floor of Monticello, showing the position of her mother's harpsichord in the parlor. (Drawing, courtesy of the Monticello Archives, Monticello)

2 John Isaac Hawkins's "portable grand" piano. (Photograph courtesy of the Musical Instruments Division, Smithsonian Institution)

when it was finished. He never quite got over being voted down on the celestina.

The harpsichord was finally placed aboard the ship *James* and eventually arrived in France. In answer to Jefferson's impatient inquiries, the Garveys at Rouen told him early in November that the ship had docked several days previously and that the harpsichord would be unloaded as soon as possible. Later in the month they told Jefferson that they had sent it to Paris by cart. He received this information with astonishment and asked them to remove the instrument from the cart and ship it by water, saying that he would gladly pay the cartage plus the water freight charges if the Garveys would change their arrangements. The Garveys replied that the river was too low, water transportation too costly, the harpsichord was well packed, and they had sent many musical instruments by cart without receiving any complaints. At last, after nearly a year and a half, the harpsichord arrived in Paris on November 11, 1787, and Jefferson had to admit that it arrived in good order.

It is possible that the celestina could be attached and detached as needed and that, after testing it, Walker kept it for further improvements and sent the harpsichord on without it. A note from Jefferson to Trumbull suggests this. However, by May 1788 Jefferson was praising the harpsichord and the celestina in a letter to his old friend Hopkinson. Walker continued trying new ways to simplify and improve his celestina and promised Jefferson his first successful new model.

During the two years that Patsy's harpsichord remained in Paris, it had the usual tunings and minor repairs. It received a new set of quills shortly before its departure from Paris and was shipped to Virginia late in 1789 in the box numbered nineteen on their baggage list. Most of the rest of their furniture stayed in Paris, since Jefferson expected to return there after settling his girls in Virginia. The harpsichord arrived at Monticello sometime in 1790. Again, the only way for it to travel from Richmond was by cart. Jefferson told the Richmond merchant who sent it to be sure to buy a half-wagonload of straw so that it would have a safe journey.

Patsy, who soon became Mrs. Thomas Mann Randolph, apparently always kept her harpsichord at Monticello regardless of where she and her husband lived. She always spent much time at Monticello looking after her father's affairs and moved there permanently after his retirement from politics. She never acknowledged that any other musical instrument was the equal of her Kirkman harpsichord, and certainly none could ever be its superior. Her daughters, Ellen and Virginia, learned to play it, Ellen far more enthusiastically than her sister. A tax inventory of family possessions listed it in 1815. As late as 1824, Nicholas Trist, Virginia's fiancé, was insisting that Virginia practice on it regularly.[38] Another Randolph sister, Cornelia, showed its location in the parlor at Monticello in a drawing she made sometime in the 1820s (illus. 1).[39] Martha Randolph probably kept the harpsichord long after it ceased to be playable. Records of the sale of furniture from Monticello do not mention it, yet Martha did not take it with her to subsequent residences at Edgehill and Washington. An unknown correspondent who visited Monticello in 1830 mentioned ". . . an old Harpsichord, whose tuneless notes mournfully reverberated as I touched the keys."[40] A family tradition of the Barclays, who bought Monticello from Jefferson's heirs, has it that Dr. Barclay found an old mahogany harpsichord in the house and, upon discovering that it was useless as a musical instrument, he took it apart and converted it into a piece of furniture for his wife.[41] Several people came to possess keys from its keyboard.[42]

Maria Jefferson Eppes got her Kirkman harpsichord in 1798. Her father noted in his account book that he had made a forty-dollar down payment on it to Harper of Philadelphia in the form of a draft on his Philadelphia agent, John Barnes.[43] He wrote to Maria's mother-in-law, asking her to tell Maria that "I have sacrificed my own judgement to her wishes and bought her a harpsichord. . . . It is one of Kirchman's [*sic*] highest priced, and of a fine silver tone; double-keyed, but not with as many pedals as her sister's."[44] He did not give

[38] [Ellen Wayles Randolph], Monticello, to Martha Jefferson Randolph, Poplar Forest, Sept. 27, 1816; [Ellen], Poplar Forest, to [Mrs. Randolph], Monticello, Aug. 18, 1817, EWC, ViU. Nicholas Trist, La Fourche, Louisiana, to Virginia Jefferson Randolph, Jan. 1 and Sept. 30, 1822; Mary Elizabeth Randolph Eppes, Poplar Forest, to Virginia Jefferson Randolph, Monticello, May 19, 1824, NPT, NcU. Tax inventory, 1815, Monticello Archives, Monticello.

[39] Cornelia Jefferson Randolph, drawing, ca. 1820s, Monticello Archives, Monticello.

[40] Monticello Archives, Monticello. This quotation is from a clipping from the Charlottesville *Virginia Advocate*, May 28, 1830, p. 2.

[41] Monticello Archives, Monticello. Excerpt from "Sketches of the Moon and Barclay Families."

[42] *Ibid.* "The Barclays at Monticello" [1831], *Apostolic Guide*, n.d.; photostat of excerpt from the *Jefferson Republican*, Charlottesville, Jan. 25, 1888, TJ Additionals, ViU.

[43] Account Books, Mar. 21, 1798.

[44] TJ, Philadelphia, to Mrs. Elizabeth Eppes, Mar. 24, 1798, TJ Papers, MHi. There is a two-manual 1798 Kirkman harpsichord, complete with Venetian swell, in the Musical Instruments Room of the Boston Museum of Fine Arts. It is in playable condition and certainly has the "fine silver tone" Jefferson mentions.

any reason for his apparent reluctance to buy Maria a harpsichord. He certainly would not have regretted having spent the money on it. It is more probable that, although he was trying to treat both daughters exactly the same, he was well aware that harpsichords were rapidly going out of fashion and he would have preferred to buy Maria a piano.

Jefferson wrote to Martha and her husband to tell them that he had bought the harpsichord for Maria, shipped it by water to Richmond, and arranged for it to be shipped again by water from Richmond to Milton, a river port close to Monticello.[45] Both Martha and her husband wrote to tell him when it arrived. Thomas Mann Randolph stated that it "did not receive the smallest injury from its double voyage, land carriage or unpacking." Martha, who paid more attention to harpsichords, said that the lock and some of the decoration was torn off. She was willing to admit that it was a good harpsichord, but of course she did not believe that it came anywhere near her own.[46]

Maria and her husband, John Wayles Eppes, did not spend as much time at Monticello as the Randolphs, but Maria seems also to have left her harpsichord there. When Jefferson wrote to tell her that her harpsichord had arrived at Monticello, he toned down Martha's comparison of the new one with her own by saying tactfully that he thought Maria's had a sweeter tone for a moderate-sized room, while Martha's was more suitable for a very large room.[47] Maria's did not have a celestina. Three years later Jefferson gave Maria her choice of the harpsichord or the Hawkins piano (see below). Maria wanted to think about it for awhile, especially if he had not promised the harpsichord to anyone else. She wanted to wait and see whether or not the piano was going to stay in tune. She feared it would not,[48] and she was right. She wisely chose the harpsichord.

Little time remained to Maria to enjoy her harpsichord or, indeed, anything else. Several years after her death in 1804, Jefferson, sorting out various Eppes possessions from the rest of the Monticello furnishings, packed up the harpsichord and shipped it to Richmond,

[45] TJ, Philadelphia, to Thomas Mann Randolph, Edgehill, Mar. 22 and Apr. 19, 1798, TJ Papers, DLC. TJ, Philadelphia, to Martha Jefferson Randolph, Edgehill, Apr. 5, 1798, Betts and Bear, *Family Letters*, pp. 159–60.

[46] Thomas Mann Randolph, Belmont, to TJ, Philadelphia, Apr. 29, 1798, EHR, ViU. Martha Jefferson Randolph, Belmont, to TJ, Philadelphia, May 12, 1798, Betts and Bear, *Family Letters*, p. 160.

[47] TJ, Philadelphia, to Maria Jefferson Eppes, May 19 and June 6, 1798, Betts and Bear, *Family Letters*, p. 163, 165–66.

[48] Maria Jefferson Eppes, Bermuda Hundred, to TJ, Washington, Feb. 2, 1801, *ibid.*, p. 194.

to be forwarded to John Wayles Eppes at Eppington. He was sure that Jack's mother would enjoy having it now, and eventually it would belong to Francis, son of Maria and Jack. Discovering that he had forgotten to pack one of the pedal rods, he gave it to an Eppes servant who called at Monticello on his way to Eppington.[49]

Many years later, Maria's son, Francis Eppes, offered the harpsichord to his grandfather for Poplar Forest. None of the Eppeses played it, and it was now at Millbrook, an Eppes property about halfway between Monticello and Poplar Forest. Francis's father repeated the offer, adding that he had even kept the box in which he had shipped the harpsichord from Eppington to Millbrook, thus simplifying transporting it to Poplar Forest. Jefferson, knowing that Martha and her daughters would enjoy having an instrument at Poplar Forest, accepted, on condition that it really still belonged to Francis and that he could have it back if he ever wanted it. In September 1820 Jefferson and his granddaughter Ellen Randolph went to Poplar Forest. They stopped on the way at Millbrook to look at the harpsichord. Ellen said that it was in dreadful shape: there was a twelve- to fourteen-inch crack in the soundboard, nearly all the strings were gone, the keys were so swollen as to render the instrument unplayable, and the metal parts of the stops were too rusty to work. There was also some music of Maria's, now moldy and tattered. Both music and harpsichord had lain in a cellar for years.[50]

Jefferson lost no time in having the damaged instrument repaired. He immediately ordered new strings from Richmond, but had trouble getting them; for since harpsichords had yielded in popularity to pianos, parts for them were difficult to find. His Richmond agent had Mr. Stoddart, a "celebrated Piano maker recently from Europe," select the strings.[51] Nowhere in Richmond could they get a complete

[49] TJ, Monticello, to John Wayles Eppes, Sept. 26, 1807, TJ Papers, ViU. TJ, Monticello, to John Wayles Eppes, Eppington, Sept. 29, 1807, TJ Papers, DLC.

[50] Francis Eppes, Millbrook, to TJ, Monticello, Dec. 28, 1819, Betts and Bear, *Family Letters*, p. 432. TJ to John Wayles Eppes, June 30, 1820, TJ Papers, ViU. [Ellen Wayles Randolph], Poplar Forest, to Martha Jefferson Randolph, Monticello, Sept. 13, 1820, EWC, ViU. John Wayles Eppes, Millbrook, to TJ, Monticello, Feb. 6 and July 8, 1820, TJ Papers, MHi.

[51] "Mr. Stoddart" was probably Robert Stodart, a Scottish pianomaker related to the famous Stodart family of pianomakers in England. He could very well have been in Richmond in 1819. He is known to have arrived in the United States in 1819 and lived here for many years, but his whereabouts are vague until he appeared in 1836 as a partner in the piano-building firm of Stodart, Worcester, and Dunham of New York City. *Grove's American Supplement*, p. 20.

set of strings, and the most they could hope for was that what they sent would prove suitable. Martha Randolph ordered an additional four dollars' worth of strings in Charlottesville. The strings arrived late in October. Unfortunately, all Jefferson's horses were sick and, as a consequence, he had to postpone the fall trip to Poplar Forest. He sent someone with a wagon to Millbrook for the harpsichord and had it brought to Monticello. Martha Randolph and John Hemings, a Monticello slave who was an expert woodworker, repaired and restrung it and got it ready to go to Poplar Forest whenever weather and horses permitted. The last mention of Maria's harpsichord is that of April 1821 when Jefferson was getting ready to go to Poplar Forest and would probably take the harpsichord. Martha would go along to tune it.[52] It must have been taken to Poplar Forest and eventually disposed of by Francis Eppes. All subsequent references to a harpsichord at Monticello are clearly to Martha's; the Randolph girls spoke frequently of "mama's harpsichord," but never of any other.

One of Jefferson's most interesting connections was with John Isaac Hawkins of Philadelphia. Hawkins was a Jack of all trades and was particularly ingenious as a mechanical tinkerer. He had at various times been a civil engineer, poet, preacher, phrenologist, and inventor of many strange devices.[53] He was also something of a composer and had invented a new musical gadget that Jefferson could not resist. "A person here," he wrote to Martha in 1800 from Philadelphia, "has invented the prettiest improvement in the Forte piano I have ever seen. It has tempted me to engage one for Monticello, partly for its excellence and convenience, partly to assist a very ingenious, modest and poor young man, who ought to make a fortune by his invention."[54] The invention was Hawkins's famous, or infamous, "portable grand," an early attempt at an upright piano. It was portable insofar as it was small enough, when closed, to look like "the underhalf of a bookcase" and could be easily moved by its handles (illus. 2).[55] To eyes accustomed to rectangular or wing-shaped keyboard instruments, with horizontal stringing, its appearance was

[52] Captain Bernard Peyton, Richmond, to TJ, Monticello, Oct. 5 and 23, 1820; TJ to Peyton, Oct. 23, 1829; TJ to John Wayles Eppes, Oct. 22, 1820, TJ Papers, MHi. Mrs. Elizabeth Trist, Farmington, to Nicholas Trist, West Point, Apr. 5, 1821, NPT, DLC. Account Books, Oct. 9 and Nov. 6, 1820.

[53] Daniel Spillane, *History of the American Pianoforte*, 1890. Reprint (New York, 1969), pp. 82–83.

[54] TJ, Philadelphia, to Martha Jefferson Randolph, Monticello, Feb. 11, 1800, Betts and Bear, *Family Letters*, pp. 183–84.

[55] *Ibid.*

unusual. Jefferson, however, was "tempted" to the amount of $264 for Hawkins's five-and-a-half octave model, which he paid for in four installments between January and May 1800.[56]

The odd-looking instrument came to Monticello in the early summer of 1800. It had been exposed to much rain, a normal hazard of eighteenth- and nineteenth-century piano transportation. Jefferson thought that it had been too well covered to sustain much damage, but it was very much out of tune. He tuned it, and everyone was so delighted with it that it was predicted that Maria would prefer it to the harpsichord. Martha preferred it to any harpsichord she had ever seen—except, of course, her own Kirkman, with its celestina.[57]

The portable grand's career was short and inglorious. After only two years, Jefferson was ready to send it back for repairs. It simply would not stay in tune, and for over a year it had even failed to stay in tune for an hour. Jefferson assured Hawkins that he had not let anyone else try to repair it, although one wonders if perhaps Jefferson himself had not worked on it a little. Hawkins was not surprised at the failure of the piano; the same thing happened to two others he built, but he was absolutely certain that he could repair all of them. He regretted that he was so short of money that Jefferson would have to pay for the repairs and shipping the piano to Philadelphia, a total of about forty dollars. Hawkins would cheerfully refund Jefferson's money upon his return from England, where he was going to claim a legacy, as soon as he could raise the money for passage.[58] In the meantime Jefferson read in a newspaper that Hawkins had invented another musical marvel, the claviol (see Chapter V). He gave Hawkins permission to sell his piano if he had a buyer and send him either a claviol or another piano in return. Hawkins noted the arrival of Jefferson's piano, not improved by another bout with wet weather, and announced that he no longer made pianos. But he happened to have one on hand, the best one he ever made, as a matter of fact, and he was willing to swap. He sent a drawing and description of the claviol, claiming that he could not possibly supply one in less than a year. A year later, confident as ever, he told Jefferson that he was going to England to start a claviol factory and that Jefferson would receive the first perfect model.[59] Apparently Jefferson never got either a claviol or another piano from him, and the claviol seems

[56] Account Books, Jan. 31, Feb. 12, Apr. 23, May 12, 1800.

[57] TJ, Monticello, to Maria Jefferson Eppes, July 4, 1800, Betts and Bear, *Family Letters*, p. 189.

[58] TJ, Washington, to John Isaac Hawkins, Philadelphia, Apr. 13, 1802, and Hawkins to TJ, Apr. 21, 1802, TJ Papers, DLC.

[59] TJ, Washington, to John Isaac Hawkins, Philadelphia, June 17, 1802,

never to have been a commercial success. Hawkins went to England and remained there until 1848.[60] Whether or not Jefferson's three-hundred-dollar investment was ever made good remains unknown.

Another Monticello piano is not so readily documented. It is on display at Monticello and was acquired through the Trist descendants. It is a lovely little Astor and Company square piano of mahogany and satinwood. Its compass is five and a half octaves. In its original form it had no legs and was supported by a stand. It is now provided with legs and its exterior has been beautifully restored, but the instrument is no longer playable. It is of a type that the Astor company built between 1799 and 1815. It does not correspond with any recorded piano purchase by Jefferson, but its price could quite easily be subsumed in some larger amount paid to one of his agents.[61] References to a piano at Monticello are vague and sporadic until Jefferson finally bought one for Virginia Randolph Trist in 1825 (see below). One visitor mentioned that when Jefferson took him into the large hall "a young lady was playing a piano-forte."[62] Martha Randolph indirectly referred to a piano when she thanked Nicholas Trist for sending her some almond paste, which would "enable me to play on the piano this winter, for never without it should I have had the courage to stretch out a claw rivalling the peacock's in color and roughness."[63]

Virginia Randolph, in several of her lengthy letters to her fiancé, Nicholas Trist, told him some local gossip involving a piano that Jefferson evidently kept for a neighbor. A Dr. Watkins, their "sole prop in sickness," was leaving for Tennessee, the move having been instigated by the fact that "his b——ch of a wife had at length prevailed." The doctor wanted to leave his wife's piano at Monticello until he got settled. The girls could not practice on it, but could "hear it once in a while." A later story either corrected or confused the first

---

and Hawkins to TJ, July 16, 1802, TJ Papers, DLC. Hawkins to TJ, June 8, 1803, TJ Papers, MHi.

60 Richard J. Wolfe, ed., *Secular Music in America 1801–1825: A Bibliography* (New York, 1964), I, 349–50.

61 Monticello Archives, Monticello. The Smithsonian Institution has an unrestored Astor fortepiano almost exactly like the one at Monticello, with a serial number of the same series. Their research enables us to date the Monticello piano ca. 1799–1815. Pamphlet published by the Division of Musical Instruments, Museum of History and Technology, "A Checklist of Keyboard Instruments at the Smithsonian Institution," pp. 2–3.

62 Adam Hodgson, *Letters from North America* (London, 1824), p. 314.

63 Martha Jefferson Randolph, Monticello, to Nicholas Trist, Donaldsonville, Louisiana, Dec. 2, 1821, NPT, DLC.

one: Virginia heard that it was the doctor who wanted to go to Tennessee and that his wife did not know he intended to stay. At any rate, the doctor brought the piano to Monticello, someone at Monticello (probably John Hemings) mended one of its legs, the girls briefly enjoyed its "silver tones" and Virginia's letters lead us to believe that the doctor finally had it shipped to Tennessee.[64]

The last of the long list of Monticello instruments was the piano that Jefferson bought in 1825 for Virginia Randolph Trist, the granddaughter who had fussed so much about not having anything but her mother's old harpsichord to practice on. Jefferson only lived for a few months after the piano came, but he would have been happy to know how faithfully and obstinately the Trists hung onto it and took it with them wherever they went for many years.

After a number of false starts, much haggling over practically nonexistant money, and a family row, Jefferson and Martha Randolph asked Joseph and Ellen (Randolph) Coolidge to get a piano for Virginia in Boston. They were permitted to spend up to $250 for it. There followed an acrimonious exchange, with Jefferson, Martha, and Nicholas on Virginia's side against "the *prudence*" of the family at Tufton, Virginia's brother Thomas Jefferson (Jeff) Randolph, and his wife Jane. Martha overrode her son's and daughter-in-law's perfectly legitimate objections to the purchase by "declaring them incompetent to the business, having no ear they could form no just calculation upon the subject."[65] Virginia was quite upset over going against the wishes of her brother Jeff, "who tells me I have no right to any amusement that will cost money" and who thought she was "on the verge of a most foolish extravagant act."[66] She wanted the piano very badly and, with her grandfather and mother backing her, she certainly had all the power on her side. Nicholas figured out a way to get the money for the piano and Virginia sent Ellen a draft for it. In the meantime, Virginia continued to practice on the harpsichord.[67]

The Coolidges were delighted to go piano-shopping for Virginia and incidentally to indulge in a little family one-upmanship by fre-

[64] Virginia Jefferson Randolph, Monticello, to Nicholas Trist, Donaldsonville, Louisiana, Feb. 23, Mar. 7, Aug. 3, and Sept. 17, 1823, NPT, DLC.

[65] Martha Jefferson Randolph, Monticello, to Ellen Wayles Coolidge, Boston, Aug. 2 and Sept. 1, 1825; Cornelia Jefferson Randolph, Monticello, to Ellen, Aug. 3, 1825, EWC, ViU.

[66] Virginia Randolph Trist, Monticello, to Ellen Wayles Coolidge, Boston, Sept. 3, 1825, EWC, ViU.

[67] Martha Jefferson Randolph, Monticello, to Ellen Wayles Coolidge, Boston, Sept. 18, 1825, EWC, ViU. Virginia Randolph Trist, Monticello, to Nicholas Trist, White Sulphur Springs, Sept. 4, 1825, NPT, NcU.

quently mentioning their own new Broadwood grand from London. They even looked at another Broadwood grand, thinking that it would be quite handy to ship it to Virginia in the box in which theirs came from London. Soon they stopped mentioning Broadwood grands and switched to praises of a Boston-made piano. Joseph Coolidge assured Nicholas Trist that if the piano he was now looking at proved to be as good as promised, few in Virginia could compare with it.[68] Ellen described it to Jefferson, praising its fine workmanship, beautiful tone, and interior structure. Coolidge shipped it to Richmond in February 1826 and anxiously awaited word of its safe arrival.[69] "If you were as anxious for its coming as we were for its going," he wrote, "your impatience must have been extreme." Coolidge asked for a song from Virginia for his labors, whenever he next saw her, and teased Nicholas as being unworthy of having a wife with such a voice. He had the pianomaker add some kind of third pedal to the piano especially for Mrs. Randolph, anticipating its effect on her improvisations.[70]

The piano came to Monticello on March 18, 1825, and was an immediate success. Jefferson told Ellen that Mrs. Cary "has exhibited to us its full powers, which are indeed great. Nobody slept the first night, nor is the tumult yet over on this the 3d day of its emplacement."[71] Every day it sounded better as they learned to bring out its clear, sweet tone. Martha Randolph wanted one like it, but of course could not afford one. Her father was so pleased with it that he said he would get one if the lottery was successful.[72]

Currier and Gilbert of Boston built the piano, and they built it at a greatly reduced price. Let Joseph Coolidge tell in his own words and underlinings the story of some slight damage to the piano and of his "deal" with the builders:

its makers know not how to explain the *impossibility* of *using the damper* pedal: every part was numbered, so that we hoped there would be no difficulty in properly adjusting them. "Currier and Gilbert" beg that this different [?] may be taken apart, and *rightly* arranged; as the power of

[68] Joseph Coolidge, Jr., Boston, to Nicholas Trist, Monticello, Sept. 27, Oct. 5, and Oct. 10, 1825, NPT, DLC.

[69] Coolidge to Martha Jefferson Randolph, Nov. 11, 1825; Virginia Randolph Trist to Ellen Wayles Coolidge, Oct. 16, 1825; Ellen to Mrs. Randolph, Jan. 2, 1826; Coolidge to Mrs. Randolph, Feb. 8, 1826, EWC, ViU. Coolidge to Nicholas Trist, Feb. 13 and Mar. 3, 1826, NPT, DLC.

[70] Coolidge to Trist, Mar. 25, 1826, NPT, DLC.

[71] TJ, Monticello, to Ellen Wayles Coolidge, Boston, Mar. 19, 1826, Betts and Bear, *Family Letters*, p. 475.

[72] Martha Jefferson Randolph, Monticello, to Joseph Coolidge, Jr., Boston, Apr. 8, 1826, EWC, ViU.

the instrument can never be known unless the wires are free. It has *damped* our pleasure a little that "Aunt Cary" did not hear it in its perfection! As allusion has been (repeatedly) made to *probable* orders for instruments—in letters from Mary and Virginia—I wish you to understand distinctly the arrangement which we made with Mr. C. and G. They are young men who are desirous of becoming known; they consented, therefore, that an instrument which they valued at $450 should be sent at a much lower price, in order to have the reputation of being selected to make a piano destined to Monticello. They now ask me for an instrument precisely similar to yours $450 and will not take less: this is because the *case* is an exclusive one, and because they have used the steel pivot throughout instead of leather; have introduced the "*back-catch*," and given the extra keys. But if they cannot make such as yours for a less sum than $450, they *can* make a faithful, good-toned, and extremely neat instrument for $250; and from this they graduate their prices, in comparison with their instruments, up to $850: they are most ingenious young men, and can be depended upon; beginning as consciencious [*sic*] as they are skillful. If therefore any orders be given, *let the amount always be stated explicitly* to which the individual is willing to go.[73]

Thomas Jefferson died July 4, 1826, and the family closed Monticello in November of that year. The Trists stayed with Jeff Randolph's family at Tufton. Martha Randolph and her two youngest children, Septimia and George, went to Boston to stay indefinitely with Ellen and Joseph Coolidge. Nicholas Trist moved Virginia's piano from Monticello to Tufton and put it in her room rather than the parlor or dining room. Knowing Jeff's aversion to music, particularly if it cost money, she probably could not have had it at Tufton at all if she had not been willing to put it in her room. Nicholas moved it safely and without incident.[74] The piano returned briefly to Monticello, with the Trists, who lived there until the family sold the property.[75]

Virginia Trist, her children, and her piano later moved to Edgehill, the new home of the Jeff Randolphs, to wait for Nicholas to get

[73] Coolidge to Nicholas Trist, Apr. 8, 1826, NPT, DLC. Timothy Gilbert and Ebenezer R. Currier were apprentices to John Osborn, who was considered the most important man in American piano-building ca. 1815–1835. Coolidge ordered TJ's piano about the time Currier and Gilbert formed a partnership and began their own business. From 1826 to 1829 they had a shop at 393 Washington St., Boston. Christine M. Ayars, *Contributions to the Art of Music in America by the Music Industries of Boston, 1640 to 1936* (New York, 1937), pp. 107, 109, 240–41.

[74] Mary Jefferson Randolph, Tufton, to Ellen Wayles Coolidge, Boston, Nov. 26, 1826, EWC, ViU. Ellen Bankhead, [Tufton], to Septimia Randolph, Boston, Dec. [1826], SRM, ViU.

[75] Virginia Randolph Trist, Monticello, to Mrs. Virginia Cary, Bremo Recess, May 2, 1828, NPT, NcU.

established in Washington, D.C., in a new job as a clerk in the State Department and to find a house for them. Nicholas had a chance to buy a very good London-made grand piano from a first-rate musician in Washington. He wondered if Virginia would consider selling hers (maybe Jeff would buy it for his girls) rather than put up with the expense and risk of moving it so far. Virginia was appalled, for no piano was as good as hers. She did not think the cost of shipping it would be prohibitive. She was somewhat worried about its safety during shipping, but a local musician/tuner had recently tuned her piano and pronounced it sturdy enough to withstand a trip to England, if necessary. Virginia's mother paid two-thirds of the fifteen-dollar tuning charge because she and Septimia had used the piano more than Virginia. Jeff, by the way, now had a piano for his girls, and it would be interesting to know just how he was persuaded to buy one. Virginia was careful to point out to Nicholas that Jeff's piano was vastly inferior to hers and cost much less.[76]

Virginia's piano traveled to Washington, but suffered much damage in transit from wet weather. Several years later, while Virginia was visiting at Edgehill, Nicholas wrote to tell her that he was considering swapping a horse and her piano for a good German grand he had heard about. Perhaps it is just as well that a written record of Virginia's reaction to this has not survived.[77]

The piano did not have much of a chance to rest quietly in Washington because by 1835 the Trists were making plans to move to Havana, Cuba, where Nicholas had been appointed consul. Acting upon Joseph Coolidge's advice, Virginia sent the piano to Boston for repairs and storage. Fortunately, she was able to send it to Currier, its original builder. She sold most of her other furniture in Washington, planning to buy new furniture in Boston and have it shipped to Cuba from there. Nicholas instructed Virginia to write immediately to Currier and tell him not to clean or restore the outer case of the piano, for it was advisable that it look like an old piece of furniture in order to avoid the very high Cuban duty on new furniture. Currier repaired and tuned the piano and sent it to Coolidge's. The Trists bought their new furniture and household goods and shipped everything by rail from Boston to Providence, then by sea to Havana.[78]

[76] Nicholas Philip Trist, Washington, to Virginia Randolph Trist, Edgehill, May 31, 1829, and Virginia to Nicholas, June 6 and Sept. 2, 1829, NPT, NcU.

[77] Virginia Randolph Trist, Washington, to Ellen Wayles Coolidge, Boston, Nov. 8, 1829, EWC (restricted box), ViU. Nicholas Trist, Washington, to Virginia Randolph Trist, Edgehill, Oct. 20, 1831, NPT, NcU.

[78] Virginia Randolph Trist, Washington, to Nicholas Trist, Havana, June

In March 1839, Virginia Trist and various children and sisters moved to St. Servan, France, leaving Nicholas in Havana to finish his job and dispose of furniture and property. Nicholas really hated to part with the piano: "so many associations! In the first place, Joseph's *brotherly* interest in procuring it, . . . then your mother's playing on it, your grandfather's listening to it, you, Pattie [the Trist's daughter], &c, &c. But it is too expensive an article to be retained by people as poor as we, merely on account of the associations."[79] Nicholas's next letter said that he had not yet sold the piano because of the Cuban habit of "beating down" the price. In France, Virginia first rented a piano for Pattie, then, with Nicholas's approval, bought one. She told Nicholas to take whatever he could get for the old piano. Virginia's younger sister, Septimia Randolph Meikleham, also lived in Cuba at that time, so Virginia suggested that perhaps Nicholas could sell the piano more easily if he had it tuned and took it to Septimia's house, where she could show it.[80]

Virginia Trist's letter of April 29, 1840, contains the last specific reference to the Boston piano. The most reasonable assumptions are that either Nicholas sold it or it stayed at Septimia's house in Havana until it fell apart from hard use and moving. The Trists had at least one other piano, perhaps two or three. Virginia brought back to Cuba the piano that she bought in France, and when the Trists finally returned to the United States they shipped it to New Orleans, to Nicholas's brother Hore Browse Trist. They had a piano, or pianos, when they again lived in Washington, but there is no evidence as to whether it was the French one or another new one. Septimia Randolph Meikleham had a piano in New York when Pattie Trist visited

---

21, 1835; Joseph Coolidge, Jr., Washington, to Nicholas Trist, Havana, rec'd July 7, 1835; Nicholas to Virginia, July 17, 1835; Railroad receipt for the Boston and Providence Railroad Corp., Oct. 17, 1836; Receipted bill from T. Gilbert and Co., Boston, to Mrs. Trist for tuning, regulating, and transporting the piano, Oct. 29, 1836, NPT, NcU. Ellen Wayles Coolidge, Boston, to Virginia Randolph Trist, Washington, Sept. 27, 1835, EWC, ViU. Martha Jefferson Randolph, Boston, to Septimia Randolph, c/o Hore Browse Trist, Donaldsonville, Louisiana, Jan. 3, 1836, SRM, ViU. The Currier and Gilbert piano-building business became Currier and Co. after 1829 (see n. 73) but operated at the same address until 1834. Coolidge's letter suggests that after 1834, Currier worked for Gilbert. T. Gilbert and Co. was at 402 Washington St., Boston, 1834–36. Ayars, 240–41.

[79] Nicholas Trist, Havana, to Virginia Trist, St. Servan, France, Mar. 7 and Mar. 17, 1839, NPT, NcU.

[80] Virginia Trist, St. Servan, France, to Nicholas Trist, Washington, Apr. 29, 1840, NPT, NcU. Septimia, visiting the Trists for health reasons, met and married Dr. David Meikleham, a Scottish physician living in Havana. They later moved to Scotland and eventually settled permanently in New York.

her in 1846, but it is quite unlikely that it was the Boston piano, moved from Cuba to New York by way of Scotland. After 1840 no other piano was called "Virginia's piano;" the family always called the Boston piano "Virginia's piano" and Nicholas, in his letters to Virginia, always called it "your piano." The other pianos were variously known as "Pattie's piano," "Aunt Tim's piano," or simply "the piano."[81] Anyone who is not a piano-lover will readily conclude that these people had a superfluity of pianos; however, it is not likely that they still had the Boston piano, "Virginia's piano," a gift of her grandfather, after 1840.

[81] Nicholas Trist, Havana, to Virginia Trist, Paris, Aug. 31, 1841; Martha J. Trist [Pattie], Edgehill, to Virginia Trist, Washington, Nov. 16, 1845; Martha J. Trist, New York, to Virginia Trist, Washington, Sept. 12, 1846, NPT, NcU.

CHAPTER V

The Mechanical Delights of a Delightful Recreation

AS AN INCURABLE and ingenious tinkerer, Jefferson derived as much pleasure from learning about technical innovations in the production of music as from the music itself. He corresponded with friends such as Francis Hopkinson and John Isaac Hawkins about many details concerning new and often peculiar things to do with keyboard instruments. A few of these things could possibly have been improvements; some were outright eccentricities. Since his lifetime coincided with the years of transition from the harpsichord to the piano, he had ample opportunity to become familiar with both instruments. His detailed descriptions of keyboard instruments indicate that he really knew quite a lot about them, probably as much as most contemporary American craftsmen. He usually tuned and repaired his own keyboard instruments or supervised while his daughter Martha or John Hemings did it. Several times he wrote down the pattern he followed in tuning. It is a pattern of fifths and octaves, very much the same as tuners use today. Eighteenth-century pitch was lower than we know it today, but the scale was tuned in even temperament.[1]

Whenever Jefferson ordered a musical instrument he always asked that extra strings, tuning forks, tuning hammers, and any other accessories he might need be included with the order. He had his friend Hopkinson recommend a craftsman in Philadelphia to make new jacks for his spinet, which he probably installed himself.[2] In 1820, when harpsichords were no longer fashionable, he still owned one that was in constant use (Martha's) and was making plans to restore a second one (Maria's). Several entries in his account books mention repairs and tuning in various towns where he lived. He was very precise in giving instructions for the packing and shipping of his instruments whenever he moved them. Martha's

[1] TJ's tuning pattern survives in two places in the Monticello music collection and on a fragment in the TJ Papers, DLC. For an excellent simple discussion of tuning, see Wolfgang Zuckerman, *The Modern Harpsichord* (New York, 1969), pp. 241–45.

[2] TJ, New York, to Francis Hopkinson, Philadelphia, Aug. 14, 1790, Boyd XVII, 390.

harpsichord came all the way from France unscathed, but in later years, despite all precautions, he received at least one rain-damaged piano.

Jefferson was interested in enlarging the compass of some types of musical instruments, although his inquiries along this line are more in the realm of wishful thinking than practicality. He was very fond of the sticcado, a "pretty little instrument" that Benjamin Franklin always carried about with him. It resembled a small dulcimer with glass bars and keys and had a three-octave compass. Jefferson wanted Hopkinson to devise a means of giving it an additional upper and lower octave having as sweet a tone as the glass bars of the middle octave.[3] He once asked John Trumbull to find a six-octave glass harmonica. Trumbull told him that such a behemoth did not exist, the biggest ones possessing only three octaves.[4] When buying pianos, he seems to have preferred the larger five-and-a-half-octave models to the more common ones of five octaves or less. His Hawkins upright was one of these larger models and so is the Astor piano presently at Monticello.

An entry in his memorandum book for 1770 is the earliest record of Jefferson's knowledge of keyboard instruments and his lifelong practice of describing exactly what he wanted. He was ordering a clavichord for Martha Wayles Skelton, and he had made a note describing the kind he thought would be best:

> clavichord—compass from Double G to F in alt. to be made for holding in the lap, or laying on a table as light and portable as possible. The wood veneered over with the finest mahogany. The keys ivory, flats and sharps tortoise shell. As few strings as possible for the compass, *i.e.*, some make one string do for 2 or 3 keys, others put a string for every key, which is not so well. To be made at Hamburgh in Germany. Plenty of spare strings wanted. Every possible precaution to prevent the rattling of the keys.[5]

In other words, he wanted a fretted clavichord having a range from the second G below middle C to the third F above. And how practical of him to want "as few strings as possible" on the instrument and plenty of spares. Jefferson leaves no indication of how he learned about clavichords, especially fretted clavichords (none are mentioned in *Virginia Gazette* advertisements), but some of his friends may have owned them.

[3] TJ, Paris, to Francis Hopkinson, Philadelphia, July 6, 1785, Boyd VIII, 263.

[4] TJ, Paris, to John Trumbull, [London], Oct. 11, 1787, and Trumbull to TJ, Oct. 30, 1787, Boyd XII, 235, 297.

[5] Memorandum Books of TJ, 1767–70, DLC.

Jefferson did not buy the clavichord. He saw a piano and immediately wrote to his London agent to change his order. Again he knew just what he wanted and described it: a solid mahogany case with no veneer, the same compass as he had specified for the clavichord, plenty of spare strings and fine workmanship, "worthy the acceptance of a lady [Martha] for whom I intend it."[6] There is no record of the actual purchase, but we have seen that he had a piano at Monticello several years later and that he might have sold it to Riedesel (see above, p. 43).

One of Jefferson's most frequent correspondents on musical gadgetry was Francis Hopkinson, a signer of the Declaration of Independence and a competent gentleman musician. John Adams described Hopkinson as "one of your pretty, little, curious, ingenious men. His head is not bigger than a large apple. . . . I have not met with anything in natural history more amusing and entertaining than his personal appearance; yet he is genteel and well-bred, and is very social."[7] Hopkinson went to considerable trouble to write about his innovations and inventions and send them to Jefferson in France; one wonders if he did this because he felt that Jefferson understood them better and was more interested in them than any of his friends in Philadelphia.

Jefferson devoted much time and thought to the purchase of a keyboard instrument for his daughter Patsy. His inclination to try anything new led him to consider buying her a piano rather than a harpsichord. His friend in Paris, the composer and pianist Piccini, advised getting a piano, for pianos were fast becoming the rage of Paris. Hopkinson preferred the harpsichord to the piano. He mentioned mutual friends in Philadelphia who had recently bought harpsichords on his recommendation and were delighted with them. Jefferson finally bought Patsy a harpsichord.

In fact, Jefferson almost had Hopkinson order him a harpsichord before he went to France. Apparently the two had discussed it because Hopkinson wrote to Robert Bremner, a London musical instrument dealer, about a harpsichord for Jefferson and sent Jefferson a copy of the letter. Jefferson had found out about a recent hybrid of harpsichord and piano, decided that he must have one, and asked Hopkinson about importing one for Patsy. He wanted the very best "double harpsichord [two keyboards] with Merlin's forte-piano Stop" and whatever else he might need to keep it in order—an extra set of

[6] TJ, Monticello, to Thomas Adams, London, June 1, 1771, Boyd I, 71–72.

[7] John Adams to Abigail Adams, Aug. 21, 1776, Lyman Butterfield, ed., *The Adams Papers*, Series II, *Adams Family Correspondence*, II (Cambridge, 1963), 104.

strings, a tuning hammer and tuning fork.[8] The "forte-piano Stop" was the brain child of one Joseph Merlin of London, and was fairly well known among people who were interested in the many current "improvements" for harpsichords. Merlin took out a patent in 1774 for "a new kind of compound harpsichord, in which, besides the jacks with quills, a set of hammers of the nature of those used in the kind of harpsichords called Piano Forte, are introduced in such manner that either may be played separately or both together at the pleasure of the performer, and for adding the aforesaid hammers to an harpsichord of the common kind already made, so as to render it such compound harpsichord."[9] Hopkinson's other correspondents did not think much of the instrument, and it is little wonder. Hopkinson told Jefferson that in the combination of the two instruments, each militated against the other so that neither was very good. Its price was about half that of either a piano or a harpsichord.[10] Jefferson never said anything more about this keyboard oddity.

The most extensive correspondence between Jefferson in Paris and Hopkinson in Philadelphia concerned Hopkinson's experiments to perfect a more efficient way of installing the quill plectra in harpsichords. The harpsichord jack carried a tongue and pivot mechanism, into which the plectrum was mounted. The plectra were usually made of crow or raven quill and were placed in a hole in the tongue of the jack. Hopkinson worked on the premise that if these quills were attached so as to afford them greater flexibility, they would not break so readily and would thus make the harpsichord easier to keep in playing condition.[11] He read his first paper on this subject to the American Philosophical Society in Philadelphia on December 5, 1783,[12] and sent Jefferson detailed drawings, directions, and models for his new method, knowing that Jefferson would be interested in it and could discuss it intelligently with him. They both hoped that Jefferson could find some instrument maker in Paris who would be willing to pay for the invention.[13]

[8] Francis Hopkinson, Philadelphia, to Robert Bremner, London, Nov. 28, 1783, copy sent to TJ in Paris, Boyd VI, 359. The original letter is in MHi.

[9] Frank Hubbard, *Three Centuries of Harpsichord Making* (Cambridge, 1965), pp. 321–22.

[10] Francis Hopkinson, Philadelphia, to TJ, Paris, Mar. 31, 1784, Boyd VIII, 57.

[11] Francis Hopkinson, Philadelphia, to TJ, Paris, May 25, 1784, Boyd VII, 285–87.

[12] Raymond Russell, *The Harpsichord and Clavichord* (London, 1949), p. 170.

[13] Francis Hopkinson, Philadelphia, to TJ, Paris, May 25, 1784, Boyd VII, 285–87.

Hopkinson commissioned a harpsichord for himself from Shudi and Broadwood of London, who allowed him thirty guineas' credit on his bill for using the new quilling method. He made further improvements on it and sent Jefferson more models and explanations, duplicates of which went to the American Philosophical Society.[14] Jefferson tried unsuccessfully to sell the new method in France. "The artisans here," he wrote to Hopkinson, "will not readily beleive [*sic*] that any thing good can be invented but in London or Paris: and to shew them the invention would be to give it up."[15] Nevertheless, Jefferson kept trying: he and Hopkinson collaborated on an advertisement early in 1785.[16]

Hopkinson eventually discarded quills as the proper material for plectra and proclaimed the superiority of leathers of different degrees of hardness, or leather-covered cork. Between 1783 and 1787 he submitted four papers on quilling to the American Philosophical Society, always sending Jefferson the same information, with models. Hopkinson found a Philadelphia craftsman who would alter harpsichords to his specifications and was exultant over their fuller and more powerful tone. He tried through another friend to sell the idea of leather plectra in England, but discovered through Jefferson that English builders were already using leather. Broadwood, of Shudi and Broadwood, asserted that leather plectra had been in use for quite some time.[17] Hopkinson's only financial reward was the credit Shudi and Broadwood gave him on his bill.

The correspondence between Jefferson and Hopkinson about many other musical curiosities and how they might or might not work is like the happy exchange between two little boys with erector sets. Hopkinson, for instance, somehow got the idea that if one could magnetize the strings of a harpsichord, the instrument would have a bigger, richer tone. He tried it on his own harpsichord and, of course, wanted Jefferson to try it. He cautioned him not to tell anyone except Benjamin Franklin about it. He sent detailed instructions; Jefferson and Franklin were to tune two unison strings of the harpsichord perfectly to each other, then rub one of them several times with a pair of magnets. The resulting tone of the magnetized string was supposed to be "much more Uniform and sweet to the

[14] Francis Hopkinson, Philadelphia, to TJ, Paris, Nov. 18, 1784, Boyd VII, 534–37.

[15] TJ, Paris, to Francis Hopkinson, Philadelphia, Jan. 13, 1785, Boyd VII, 602.

[16] Boyd VIII, 6–7.

[17] Russell, pp. 170–78.

Ear." A "judicious Ear" would "acknowledge the Effect," but in case the ear was not judicious the "operation can do no Harm, and I believe the idea is original."[18] Jefferson and Franklin never got around to trying this original idea. Franklin was too busy trying to get ready to leave Paris. Jefferson said he did not try it because he could not play the harpsichord.[19] One wonders if Jefferson was only using a tactful means to avoid disappointing his friend by telling him that the experiment was not valid. After all, he knew how to tune a harpsichord and he had a daughter who could play one.

Many eighteenth-century craftsmen were trying to develop ways to play the shivery-sounding and rather messy glass harmonica with keys instead of wet fingers. Hopkinson and Jefferson were very interested; inevitably Hopkinson tried to invent a glass harmonica with keyboard, and he and Jefferson exchanged progress reports. Hopkinson had "little Doubt of Success," even though no one in England or France had succeeded in producing a practical, salable model. Jefferson was so enthusiastic about the project that he told Hopkinson his contribution of a keyed glass harmonica would be the "greatest present which has been made to the musical world this century, not excepting the Piano forte." Hopkinson eventually made such an instrument, fitted out with keys attached to artificial fingers, and later still one that had keys with cushioned pads. Whatever touched the glass bells of the instrument, however, still had to be wet. Hopkinson could not devise a means of accomplishing this, and apparently Jefferson had no suggestions. Hopkinson finally abandoned the keyed glass harmonica, but, undaunted, turned his attention to a new invention he called the bellarmonic, which had metal bells instead of glass and required no water.[20]

Jefferson called Hopkinson's attention to a new musical gadget, told him where he would find it described and added his own refinements. Renaudin of Paris had invented a forerunner of the metronome. He had made two models, each equipped with a mainspring and balance wheel. Jefferson requested Renaudin to make him one of the second, and cheaper, variety. It had "a dial plate like that of a clock on which are arranged in a circle the words Largo, Adagio,

[18] Francis Hopkinson, Philadelphia, to TJ, Paris, Mar. 20, 1785, Boyd VIII, 50, 52.

[19] TJ, Paris, to Francis Hopkinson, Philadelphia, July 6, 1785, Boyd VIII, 263.

[20] Francis Hopkinson, Philadelphia, to TJ, Paris, June 28, 1786, Boyd X, 48; Apr. 14 and July 8, 1787, Boyd XI, 289, 562; TJ to Hopkinson, Dec. 23, 1786, Boyd X, 625.

Andante, Allegro, Presto. The circle is moreover divided into 52 equal degrees. Largo is at 1, Adagio at 11, Andante at 22, Allegro at 36 and Presto 46. Turning the index to any one of these, the pendulum (which is a string with a ball hanging to it) shortens or lengthens so that one of it's [*sic*] vibrations gives you a crotchet for that movement."[21]

Jefferson decided that he could greatly simplify the device and tell any musician how to make one for himself. Renaudin did not have the device set to indicate each tempo as a specific number of beats per minute, but Jefferson figured out how to do this. Once he assigned a number of beats per minute of each tempo, he made a very simple pendulum arrangement to give the beat and told Hopkinson how to make one. A harpsichordist could put one on his wall or on the side of his harpsichord, the violinist could hang one on his music stand: "In the wall of your chamber, over the instrument drive 5 little brads as 1.2.3.4.5. In the following manner, take a string with a bob to it, of such length as that hung on No. 1, it shall vibrate 52 times in a minute. Then proceed by trial to drive No. 2 at such a distance that drawing the loop of the string to that, the part remaining between 1 and the bob shall vibrate 60 times in a minute, fix the third for 70 vibrations &c. The cord always hanging over No. 1."[22] Jefferson's "metronome" was not automatic, but it indicated the tempo of a piece long enough for the performer to get started.

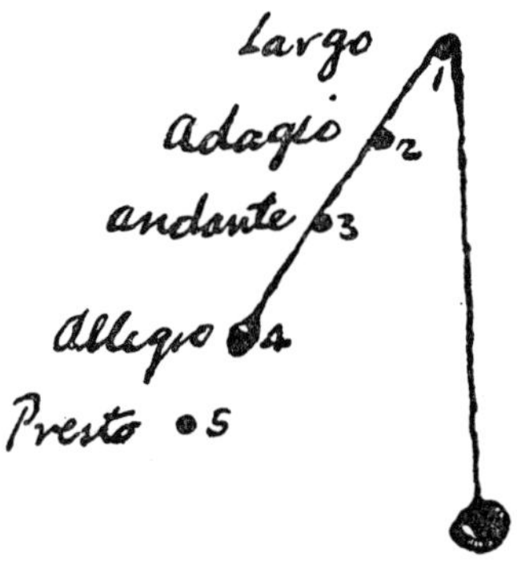

Fig. 1 Jefferson's metronome

Musical craftsmen produced several kinds of pedal keyboard instruments, which were usually used as practice instruments for organists or played in combination with a piano, harpsichord, or clavichord. Jefferson saw one in Paris and studied it closely enough to be able to sketch and describe it to Hopkinson. Jefferson called it a foot-bass and said that Johann Krumpholz invented it. According to Jefferson's little drawing, it looked rather like a king-sized clavichord, although it must have had hammers instead of tangents. Jefferson described it as:

[21] TJ, Paris, to Francis Hopkinson, Philadelphia, Jan. 3, 1786, Boyd IX, 147.

[22] *Ibid.*

a Piano forte about 10 feet deep, 18 inches broad and 9 I [inches] deep. It is of one octave only, from Fa to Fa. The part where the keys are, projects at the side in order to lengthen the levers of the keys, thus

Fig. 2 Jefferson's drawing of a foot-bass

It is placed on the floor, and the harpsichord or other piano forte is set over it, the foot acting in concert on that while the fingers play on this. There are three unison chords to every note, of strong brass wire, and the lowest have wire wrapped on them as the lowest in the piano forte. The chords give a fine, clear, deep tone, almost like the pipe of an organ.[23]

While in Paris, Jefferson bought a mechanical musical gadget that was quite common in his day, but would now be regarded as an oddity for collectors—a bird organ, for which he paid eighteen francs.[24] A bird organ was very small, about six inches square, and worked on the principle of a barrel organ. Activated by turning a small handle, it was used to teach pet birds to sing simple tunes.[25] Tradition says that the Jefferson household usually contained pet birds of one kind or another. We know nothing definite about them and find nothing more about his bird organ, but we do know from contemporary sources that he could have known about them long before he went to France.[26]

He was also interested in aeolian harps, but there is no recorded purchase of one in his account books. He had an article on them copied from the *Journal Allemand* at some point during his stay in France. The article described the instruments in rather florid detail, explaining how to set the strings advantageously, and how best to place one in a room to get the full benefit of air currents. The article also specified available sizes, styles, and prices, adding that "he who orders 5 gets the 6th free."[27]

[23] TJ, Paris, to Francis Hopkinson, Philadelphia, Dec. 23, 1783, Boyd X, 625–26.

[24] Account Books, January 24, 1785.

[25] David Tallis, *Music Boxes: A Guide for Collectors* (New York, 1971), p. 75.

[26] Lord Dunmore imported one into Virginia in 1773. Jane Carson, *Colonial Virginians at Play* (Williamsburg, 1965), pp. 100–1.

[27] Notes on aeolian harps, TJ Papers, DLC. For translating this and many other articles from French, I thank Miss Mary Faith Pusey, Manuscripts Department, ViU, and Mrs. Lucia Goodwin, Lexington, Virginia. An aeolian

When Jefferson ordered Patsy's harpsichord from Kirkman, he could not resist encumbering it with another kind of mechanical gadget that he saw during his visit to England. This was Adam Walker's celestine stop (also called a celestine apparatus or a celestina), one of several kinds of *sostenente* instruments. The purpose of the *sostenente* experiments was to produce a sustained tone, such as that of an organ or violin, on a plucked-string instrument not normally capable of producing such an effect. Walker's celestina was a distant cousin of the hurdy-gurdy and John Isaac Hawkins's claviol (see pp. 74–75), both *sostenente* experiments. Jefferson could well have known of these contrivances long before he saw Walker's invention. Roger Plenius, a London harpsichord builder, experimented with them, and both his experiments and his instruments were well known in America.[28]

One of the earliest and most famous descriptions of a *sostenente* keyboard instrument is the *Geigenwerk* described by Michael Praetorius in his *Syntagma Musicum*. In place of jacks, it had several rosined wheels kept in motion by a treadle. Depressing the key brought its string in contact with the revolving wheel and produced a bowed-string sound. Praetorius, in his description of the *Geigenwerk*, quoted its advantages from a little booklet written in 1610 by its inventor, who explained wittily and at length all the ways in which his instrument could continue a sound indefinitely and moderate it dynamically. Among other advantages, the varied sounds of the *Geigenwerk* "can be used to please women and children who otherwise do not greatly care for music—and also for the amusement of very respectable people when they are a little tipsy from a good drink."[29]

Walker's celestina must surely have delighted Jefferson's gadget-loving heart. Modern craftsmen and historians of keyboard instruments have not located any drawings of it, or any better descriptions of it than the one which Jefferson carefully wrote out in a letter to Hopkinson:

---

harp is a narrow oblong box with gut strings placed lengthwise across bridges at either end. It is placed where currents of air can activate the strings, thus producing a variety of different musical sounds.

[28] For a discussion of several of these devices, see Grove VII, 974, "Sostenente Pianoforte."

[29] Michael Praetorius, *Syntagma Musicum, 1615–20*, facsimile edition published by Barenreiter, 1958. Vol. II, *De Organographia*, 1st and 2nd parts, English trans. by Harold Blumenfeld (New Haven, 1949), pp. 67–72. Copy of translation in Music Division, DLC.

A band of single silk thread is made to pass over a pulley on the right and another on the left, so that one string of the band is almost in contact with the strings of the harpsichord. It is kept in motion by a treadle as in a flax wheel. A set of hammers is placed just above the band, and one end of each hammer being thrust up by its corresponding jack, the other is pressed down on the band, between the two unison strings of that noted, so as to make it strike them and no others. The band being always in motion, it is as if you drew a fiddle bow over those strings, and produces a tone as different from the ordinary one of the harpsichord, as is that of the violin. To prevent the pressure of the hammer from impeding the motion of the band, a friction wheel is placed tranversely in the end of every hammer, precisely in the point of contact. The whole can be shifted out of the way by a touch of the foot, and leaves the harpsichord in it's usual state. It suits slow movements, and as an accompaniment to the voice can be fixed in any harpsichord.[30]

Jefferson ordered the celestina, hoping that by the time the harpsichord was ready for it Walker would have devised a way to activate it with a spring or weight rather than by foot or hand.[31] He encountered some trouble from Kirkman, who did not like Walker's stop and did not want the thing on one of his harpsichords. He objected to it on the grounds that the resin used on the silk band clogged the wheels and stuck to the strings.[32] Jefferson suggested that the strings and wheels could simply be wiped free of resin, and wondered again if the whole apparatus could not be activated by some other means than a pedal.[33] Dr. Charles Burney, supervising the construction of the harpsichord and the installation of the celestina, kept Jefferson posted on Walker's progress. Walker, having discussed the stop with Jefferson, was eager to try his suggestions about a clockwork mechanism. After several disappointments he finally achieved a workable model, which was "perfectly sweet" and did not "produce a *Scream* by over pressure of the keys."[34] Walker modified the

[30] TJ, Paris, to Francis Hopkinson, Philadelphia, May 9, 1786, Boyd IX, 482–83. A modern harpsichord builder, Mr. E. O. Witt of Three Rivers, Michigan, believes that a dedicated gadgeteer could build a celestina from Jefferson's description. As Mr. Witt says, "except for the principle, the mechanical reconstruction rests on little else than that perhaps there's a bit of the Adam Walker in myself—I know that mentality." Jefferson obviously had "that mentality" and probably had a wonderful time keeping the celestina in proper working order over the years.

[31] TJ, Paris, to John Paradise, London, May 25, 1786, Boyd IX, 579.

[32] Dr. Charles Burney, London, to TJ, Paris, June 19, 1786, enclosed in John Paradise, London, to TJ, Paris, June 27, 1786, Boyd X, 75–76.

[33] TJ, Paris, to Dr. Charles Burney, London, July 10, 1786, Boyd X, 118.

[34] Dr. Charles Burney, London, to TJ, Paris, Jan. 20, 1787, Boyd XI, 58–59.

mechanism once more so that the instrument could survive transportation. He sent a letter giving detailed instructions on how to activate the stop, some suggestions for performing with it, a supply of extra silk bands with instructions for applying resin to them and instructions for removing the machinery from the harpsichord.[35] Later comments by Jefferson and Martha attest to the fact that the celestina was something quite special and that Martha used it for many years.

John Isaac Hawkins of Philadelphia and Thomas Jefferson became involved with each other about a piano and exchanged several lively and interesting letters over a period of years. Hawkins, an Englishman by birth, patented in 1800 an upright piano he called a "portable grand." Hawkins was not primarily a maker of musical instruments, although he had some musical talent and a natural gift for mechanics in addition to some musical training. His little pianos were musically worthless—their value lay in the fact that Hawkins was one of the first to build pianos with a metal frame, bracing, wrest-pin block, and bridge, with the tuning pins set like screws in threaded sockets.[36] Jefferson could not resist buying one (see Chapter IV for details of his misfortunes with it). He kept hoping, however, that Hawkins would either repair it or send him a replacement. Hawkins only built a few pianos and did not stay in the piano business long. Charles Willson Peale, another good friend of Jefferson, thought that Hawkins's "ingenious mechanical powers will be of great advantage to America if we can keep him."[37] Hawkins once wrote a letter of introduction to Jefferson for a musical friend of his, who supposedly played the violin very well and had "composed several beautiful beautiful pieces of music in a peculiar style."[38] No further correspondence tells us whether or not Jefferson had the privilege of becoming acquainted with the friend and his peculiar style.

Jefferson was interested in another of Hawkins's musical inventions, the claviol, and probably would have bought one had it ever been available. For several years he hoped that Hawkins would furnish him one as a replacement for the unfortunate little upright piano. The claviol worked from a ringbow mechanism with a horsehair loop. A foot pedal made the loop revolve, and keys activated

[35] Adam Walker, London, to TJ, Paris, Aug. 20, 1787, Boyd XII, 47–49.

[36] Wolfe I, 349–50; Spillane, pp. 29–30, 82–83; Loesser, p. 461.

[37] Charles Willson Peale, Philadelphia, to TJ, Washington, Jan. 10, 1803, DLC. Hawkins's "ingenious mechanical powers" had thus far produced a polygraph, a physiognotrace, and a method for "improving" rum and whiskey.

[38] John Isaac Hawkins, Philadelphia, to TJ, Washington, June 8, 1803, MHi.

sliders that drew the instrument's gut strings against the revolving loop. Hawkins rapturously described it to Jefferson:

A single note on it is much stronger than the correspondent note on a Violin or Violoncello; so much so, that a full chord taken by both hands is judged to be as Powerful as 12 or 15 violins and basses. The loud sound at a distance is similar to that of a full band, in which the hearer imagines he can distinguish Clarinetts, Violins, Horns, Basses, and indeed almost every kind of musical instrument; but near, it resembles the Organ. The Piano of it is extremely soft and sweet, and has been pronounced equal to the harmonica. The Crescendo and diminuendo is Perfect.

There are some imperfections in the machinery of that claviol which is finished in consequence of various alterations it has undergone that would render it almost useless to anyone but myself. I cannot therefore offer it for sale.[39]

Within the next year Hawkins returned to England hopeful, for several years, that he might begin manufacturing claviols and promising Jefferson the first perfect one. He never seems to have gotten very far with it, however, and eventually others appropriated his ideas.[40] A contemporary encyclopedia laconically stated: "We have never heard or seen this instrument . . . and only give this account of it as an advertisement. If its perfections are not exaggerated, its invention would be a valuable discovery."[41] One concludes that its perfections were indeed exaggerated.

Family tradition has it that the two music stands and the music rack presently at Monticello were made there by John Hemings after Jefferson's designs. The music rack is of a type often called a canterbury, with four compartments for music and a lower open shelf. One of the music stands is a rather ordinary adjustable rectangular stand on a shaft with a tripod base. The second stand looks as if only Jefferson could have designed it, although the workmanship is not of the best. It is a revolving stand with five adjustable music rests, and it folds up to make a small, neat box. When opened, it accommodates

[39] John Isaac Hawkins, Philadelphia, to TJ, Washington, July 16, 1802, DLC.

[40] Grove VII, 974.

[41] Abraham Rees, *Dr. Rees's New Cyclopaedia* . . . (Philadelphia, 1810), Vol. IX, Part 1, n. p. One wonders if TJ ever heard about Hawkins's experiments to "improve" the violin by increasing its volume. Hawkins took the back completely off a violin and placed a firm wooden bar under its breast, with a spring under the soundpost to resist the string tension. The result did produce a much louder tone, but reputedly a very bad one. Peter Davidson, *The Violin: Its Construction Theoretically and Practically Treated* (London, 1881), p. 30.

four seated players and one standing (illus. 3). Although we know that Jefferson bought music desks in Paris, the articles at Monticello are obviously handmade and do not correspond to these purchases.[42]

[42] Monticello Archives, Monticello; Account Books, Oct. 13, 1788.

CHAPTER VI

The Monticello Family's Music Collection

THE MUSIC LIBRARY of Thomas Jefferson was a functional, utilitarian, and heterogenous collection that reflected nearly three-quarters of a century of American musical taste. The earliest items he acquired were arrangements for violin (or other solo instrument) and figured bass, scores of ballad operas, light and graceful vocal music of the type popular in English pleasure garden concerts, and several "how-to" books. The period of his residence in France witnessed the acquisition of more instrumental music, keyboard music for his daughters, and many vocal selections from the opera and concert repertory. As his daughters and granddaughters became more proficient on keyboard instruments, learned to play the guitar, and sang, the collection began to include more keyboard music, many more songs, and a number of guitar books. The granddaughters, educated to the tastes of their mother and grandfather, combined an appreciation for their mother's French music, much of it in manuscript, with a liking for the rather saccharine popular songs of their own time.

Jefferson and his family acquired their music library just as anyone else does: they bought music, traded it with friends, and received it as gifts. Correspondence and account book entries fail to document, even approximately, the considerable amount of music they possessed. When Jefferson was not actually selecting and buying music himself, he was encouraging the girls to buy it; every time they left home they received requests to bring back new music. Jefferson had several sheaves of music bound into volumes. A typical account notes that in September 1801 he received a bill for thirty-four dollars for "Binding 17 Vols Demy folio Music Books, Lett'd g" from a Georgetown bookbinder.[1]

Occasionally, selections from the family music library appear among the mementos treasured by Jefferson's descendants. Appendix II lists all the music given to the Thomas Jefferson Memorial Foundation and deposited either in the University of Virginia Library or

[1] Account with John March, Georgetown, Item 5721, CSmH.

the Monticello Archives for safekeeping.[2] Unfortunately, a large part of the Jefferson music library was destroyed by a servant of one of Jefferson's descendants. The servant, who was supposed to start his mistress's parlor fire with newspapers, kept the newspapers and used the music instead. He had burned most of the music before this substitution was discovered.[3]

The oldest items in the Jefferson music library are probably the two manuscript music books that presumably belonged to Martha Wayles Jefferson and a bound volume inscribed with the name of her father, John Wayles. Mrs. Jefferson's little music books contain many songs and selections from instrumental works typical of the mid-eighteenth century and popular wherever secular music was enjoyed. The John Wayles volume consists of several books of songs and many pieces of sheet music, all bound together. The songs are typical vocal favorites of the period, full of references to shepherds and shepherdesses, figures from classical mythology, and lovely ladies and pleading swains. Also included are a number of drinking songs, but very genteel drinking songs. There are several selections from the ballad opera *Love in a Village*, which Jefferson undoubtedly saw in Williamsburg. According to the manuscript catalogue of his library (see below, and Appendix I), he owned the score of this opera at one time.

There are many references in the family correspondence to music that friends and relatives sent to Monticello. Jefferson's friend Baron Geismar, on his way home to Germany in 1780, wrote to thank Jefferson for his efforts in helping him obtain a parole and to tell him that "Doriano has all my musick for you."[4] The two friends corresponded for several years and may have exchanged other music. In 1789 Jefferson sent Geismar a "pretty little popular tune which will amuse you for a day or two."[5] The girls received music from friends, too. Lady Caroline Tufton, one of Patsy's school friends, sent her some fashionable country dances from London.[6]

Francis Hopkinson sent his little book of songs to the Jeffersons in

[2] For aid of various kinds in writing this chapter, I thank the following persons: Professor Eugene Leahy, Department of Music, University of Notre Dame; Mrs. Donald (Carolyn) B. Nolan, Roanoke, Va. (see Bibliography); Mr. David Tetrault, harpsichordist, University of Virginia; Mrs. Marshall Smelser, South Bend, Indiana.

[3] Marie Kimball, *Jefferson: The Road to Glory, 1743 to 1776* (New York, 1943), p. 59.

[4] Geismar, New York, to TJ, [Nov. ?, 1780], Boyd IV, 173.

[5] TJ to Geismar, Feb. 23, 1789, Boyd XIV, 583.

[6] Caroline Tufton, London, to Martha Jefferson Randolph, Mar. 21, 1791, EHR, ViU.

Paris as a gift for Patsy. He had told them that he was composing some songs with harpsichord accompaniment that were so easy "any Person who can play at all may perform them without much Trouble."[7] When he finished the songs and the book was published, he sent Patsy a copy. He called particular attention to the last song in the book: "The last Song, if play'd very slow, and sung with Expression, is forcibly pathetic, . . . Both Words and Music were the Work of an hour in the height of a Storm. But the Imagination of an Author who composes from his Heart, rather than his Head, is always more heated than he can expect his readers to be."[8] The "forcibly pathetic" song was about a lost traveler, and it made Polly Jefferson cry when her sister Patsy sang it to her own accompaniment on the harpsichord (surely with the celestine stop).[9]

Thomas Jefferson, at a time when his head was not completely in control of his heart, sent Maria Cosway a copy of "Jour heureux," from the opera *Dardanus*, which they may have seen together in Paris. "I send you the song I promised" he wrote. "Bring me in return its subject, *Jours heureux!*"[10] It was only a brief two months later that Maria sent him a book of Italian songs for voice and harp that she had composed, and had just had printed. Jefferson barely acknowledged them, mentioning that "I am sure they are charming,

[7] Francis Hopkinson, Philadelphia, to TJ, Paris, Oct. 23, 1788, Boyd XIV, 33.

[8] Francis Hopkinson, Philadelphia, to TJ, Paris, Dec. 1, 1788, Boyd XIV, 324.

[9] TJ, Paris, to Francis Hopkinson, Philadelphia, Mar. 13, 1789, Boyd XIV, 649. Hopkinson dedicated this book of songs to George Washington and sent him a copy of it in December 1788, at the same time he sent Jefferson's copy to Paris. Because the Delaware and Potomac rivers were frozen over, Washington, at Mt. Vernon, received his copy about the same time Jefferson received his. Washington and Hopkinson exchanged witty letters about the songs, in which they debated whether the songs might not have melted the ice on the river if music could really do all the things attributed to it by the ancients. Washington said that although he could not play or sing the songs, the "one argument which will prevail with persons of true taste" was that he could say that Mr. Hopkinson wrote them. Hopkinson replied with more classical witticisms, then asked to be appointed to the Admiralty in the new government. Francis Hopkinson to George Washington, Dec. 1, 1788, George Washington Papers, University of Pennsylvania; George Washington to Francis Hopkinson, Feb. 5, 1789, John C. Fitzpatrick, ed., *The Writings of George Washington* (Washington, D.C., 1939), XXX, 196–97; Francis Hopkinson to George Washington, Mar. 3, 1789, George Washington Papers, DLC.

[10] TJ, Paris, to Maria Cosway, Oct. 13, 1786, Boyd X, 459. There is a copy of a French edition of "Jour heureux" in the surviving Jefferson family music. See Appendix II, Part 5.

and I thank you for them."[11] He kept the songs, but made no further comment on them. They are not particularly distinguished and they do not possess Hopkinson's melodic grace.

A comparison of a list of operas Jefferson probably saw in Paris with indexes of his music collection shows that he and the girls enjoyed selections from these operas for many years. The granddaughters could only have learned to know this music well from their mother's and grandfather's music collection, yet several of these operatic numbers appear over and over in their manuscript music books. They must have liked the songs very much indeed to have spent so much time and effort copying them. A good example is the opera *Blaise et Babet* (Dezède-Morel), for which Jefferson bought tickets on September 26, 1785. Selections from this opera appear in three places in the music library: a printed edition of one of the songs and two manuscript copies in the granddaughters' music. An air from *La Fausse Magie* (Grétry-Marmontel) appears in one of Virginia Randolph Trist's manuscript music books. Selections from *Dardanus* (Sacchini), *Zémire et Azor* (Grétry-Marmontel), *Nina* (Dalayrac-Marsollier), *La Caravane du Caire* (Grétry-Morel-Comte de Provence), *Didon* (Piccini-Marmontel), and many others are also scattered through the collection, both in printed editions and in manuscript. Grétry and Piccini appear to have been favorite composers.

During his two terms as President, Jefferson was the recipient of a number of poems and songs written in his honor. Michael Fortune, author of several of them, expressed his opinion of the importance of political songs: "As it is the duty of every good Citizen to support a wise and virtuous administration by conciliating the minds of the people, it is also the Province of the Poet to promote Union by Means of Harmony."[12] Charles Willson Peale sent Martha Randolph "a piece of Music composed by Mr. Hawkins, the person whose patent Piano she is in possession of; its effect may perhaps be improved from associating the two circumstances."[13] This was, of course, John Isaac Hawkins, of piano and claviol fame. He wrote the "piece of Music" for "the Celebration of the 4th of March 1801" and named it "The People's Friend." The words were written "by a Citizen," who was Peale's son Rembrandt.

Thomas Jefferson's granddaughters Ellen and Virginia added quite a lot of music to the family library. Besides recopying family

[11] TJ, Paris, to Maria Cosway, Dec. 24, 1786, Boyd X, 627.

[12] Michael Fortune, Philadelphia, to TJ, Washington, June 23, 1801, DLC.

[13] Charles Willson Peale, Philadelphia, to TJ, Washington, Mar. 8, 1801, DLC.

favorites from their mother's music and from that of friends, they bought new music when they traveled. Among the later acquisitions were new editions of familiar old songs, songs from ballad operas, the Scotch and Irish songs that Jefferson enjoyed in his old age, keyboard music and guitar books. Ellen was most frequently commissioned as a buyer of music. Mama once asked Virginia for several things from Richmond, "and don't forget any pretty musick that comes in your way."[14]

Almost the entire Jefferson music collection is secular in nature. The little Daniel Purcell book of psalms is the only book of religious music. "St. David's Tune" was a favorite of Jefferson's, and he has written into it the words from the new metrical version of the Psalms by Tate and Brady.[15] A few hymns appear in the manuscript music books belonging to his wife, daughters, and granddaughters. Among them are several psalms, "Adeste Fideles," and the Pleyel hymn "Children of the Heavenly King."

Jefferson lost his first library in the fire at Shadwell in 1770.[16] We do not know what music he had in that library, but we may suppose that he had many other items besides the minuets consumed by rats (see above, p. 14). He undoubtedly had a head full of country fiddle tunes for which he did not need written music. We know that he carried his kit around with him, and he probably would have had with it some music that thus escaped the fire. He surely began replacing both his books and music immediately after the fire. He does not list any music purchases in the account books after the fire until a visit to Philadelphia in 1775, but in 1773 he noted that he had 1,256 volumes, not including "vols. of Music, nor my books in Williamsburg."[17]

When he began to collect his second library (which he sold to Congress in 1815), Jefferson kept a manuscript catalogue of it. This is usually called the Catalogue of 1783 because he dated it March 6, 1783. He noted that his library contained 2,640 volumes in 1783, that he had checked the volumes he already owned, and that he intended

[14] Martha Jefferson Randolph, Monticello, to Virginia Jefferson Randolph, Richmond, Apr. 23, 1819, NPT, NcU. See also: [Ellen Wayles Randolph], Washington, to Virginia [Jefferson Randolph], Monticello, Feb. 28, 1816; [Ellen Wayles Randolph], Washington, to [Martha Jefferson Randolph], Monticello, Mar. [?], 1816; [Ellen Wayles Randolph], Richmond, to [Martha Jefferson Randolph], Monticello, Apr. 9, 1819, all in EWC, ViU.

[15] Carolyn Galbraith Nolan, "Thomas Jefferson: Gentleman Musician" (M.A. thesis, University of Virginia, 1967), p. 123, n. 8.

[16] William Peden, "Some Notes Concerning Thomas Jefferson's Libraries," *William and Mary Quarterly* 1 (1944): 267.

[17] Account Books, June 22, 1775; Aug. 4, 1773.

to procure the ones not checked (see illus. 4). He obviously added to the catalogue extensively, other sections of it being much more extensively revised than the music section. E. Millicent Sowerby, who did the definitive edition of the catalogue of Jefferson's library, believes that this 1783 manuscript contains entries of items purchased as late as 1814, and that Jefferson did not take it to Europe with him, but updated it on his return.[18] Sowerby cites still another manuscript catalogue, similar in form to the Catalogue of 1783 but much smaller, and says that internal evidence suggests that this second catalogue is a list of items acquired by purchase or gift in Europe. Jefferson included the prices of some of the items in it, a practice he did not follow in the original. Upon his return from Europe he interpolated entries from the second catalogue into the original.[19]

The general form Jefferson followed in his catalogue was to divide the library topically into chapters and to make his original entries on the verso of each leaf. In the Catalogue of 1783, he devoted three chapters to his music library. They are: Chapter 35, "Music Theory"; Chapter 36, "Vocal"; and Chapter 37, "Instrumental." In the catalogue kept in Europe, he neither grouped the musical items into separate chapters nor itemized them as precisely as he did in the first catalogue; he simply lumped them with gardening, architecture, sculpture, and painting in chapters 31–37. He listed only seven items under music in the European Catalogue, although everything points to the fact that he must have bought far more than seven items. His interpolations of the European and other acquisitions into the Catalogue of 1783 are made in much less regular handwriting and are in a different color ink from the original entries. They appear on the recto of each leaf, while the original entries are on the verso. The seven items he listed in the second catalogue are:

	Rivoluzioni del teatro musicale Italiano dal Arteaga 3 v. 8vo		
	Pugnani's solos op. 3		7—4
	Pugnani's trios op. 10		7—4
	Campioni's Sonatas Op. 1, Paris		7—4
	Campioni's Sonatas Op. 6, Walsh, London.		
36.	Beggar's opera	4to	1/3
	Pleyel		

[18] E. Millicent Sowerby, comp., *Catalogue of the Library of Thomas Jefferson* (Washington, D.C., 1955), V, 215.

[19] *Ibid.*, 221–22. The originals of both of these catalogues are in the Coolidge Collection, MHi. Photostats of the Catalogue of 1783 are in DLC and ViU. The European Catalogue is on reel #27 (undated) of the microfilm of the Coolidge Collection. Both DLC and ViU have this film. I was able to examine the originals of both of these catalogues.

3 Thomas Jefferson's music stand. (Photograph courtesy of the Monticello Archives, Monticello)

v. Corelli's Solos. by Cooke.
v. Corelli's Solos. op. 5.
v. Vivaldi's Solos. op. 2.
v. Tessarini's solos. op. 2. } 1. vol. fol.
v. Wodizka's solos.
v. Campioni's & Chabran's soles.
v. Geminiani's 12. solos. op. 1.
v. Degiardino's 12. solos. } 1. vol. fol.
v. Degiardino's 6. harpsichord sonatas. op. 3.
v. Burgess's lessons for the harpsichord.
v. Boccherini's Sonatas for the harpsichord. } 1. vol. fol.
v. Felton's Concertos op. 1.
v. Stamitz' concertos for the harpsichord.
v. Bremner's harpsichord miscellany.
v. Hardin's lessons for the harpsichord.
v. Abel's Overtures. } 1. vol. fol.
v. Periodical Overtures for the harpsichord.
v. Heron's voluntaries
[illegible]'s Sonatas Op. 10.
v. Arnold's Sonatas. for the harpsichord. } 1. vol.
v. Love in a village
Handel's Lessons.
Lully's lessons.
Felton's lessons.
Stanley's solos.
v. Geminiani's minuet
v. Minuets, country dances &c. several books
v. Thumoth's English, Scotch, & Irish airs.
v. Thumoth's Scotch & Irish airs.
v. Pocket companion for the German flute 8vo.

4 A page in Jefferson's handwriting from the Catalogue of 1783

He evidently made a mark through each title as he acquired it.[20]

In Chapter 35 of the Catalogue of 1783, "Music Theory," all the entries are neatly written on the verso of the leaf, indicating that Jefferson had those items that are checked when he began keeping the catalogue.[21] That the Arteaga work was a later addition is obvious; it is entered alone on the recto of the next leaf in much less careful handwriting and a different color ink, and with a different kind of checkmark. The fact that it is in the European Catalogue supports the other evidence of its being a later addition. All the entries that Jefferson checked as being in his library, except the tutor for German flute, went to the Library of Congress where they remain today in the Rare Book Room.[22] There is no explanation for the omission of the flute tutor; perhaps Jefferson kept it for the grandchildren and the Trist boys to use in learning to play the flageolet.

The first three entries under Chapter 35—the Holden, Jackson, and Bremner works—are all typical and well-known volumes on music theory in the eighteenth century. The Jackson item is a large chart mounted on linen and folded into a quarto-size binding. Jefferson's listing "The Same" (with no checkmark) under it in his catalogue refers to a possible text that might have accompanied it but which he apparently never bought. The Burney and Arteaga volumes were books of music history and criticism. Since Jefferson owned the Burney volumes before he went to Europe, they were undoubtedly valuable sources of musical knowledge that he acquired before sailing.[23] Other items on the page are "how-to" books; Jefferson himself must surely have used the violin tutors of Francesco Geminiani and Carlo Zuccari, and Martha Randolph and her girls must have used the harpsichord tutors and Pasquali's treatise on thoroughbass. Miss Ford's volume was the best-known tutor for musical glasses. Since Jefferson never bought a set of musical glasses or a glass harmonica, he obviously did not need the book and did not buy it.[24] The Hoegi volume is a book on composition that shows the amateur composer

[20] TJ, undated holograph book catalogue, presumed to be a catalogue of acquisitions during Jefferson's residence in France. Original, MHi; available on microfilm, reel #27 (undated) of Coolidge Collection, ViU.

[21] See Appendix I for a transcription of the Catalogue of 1783.

[22] Sowerby describes them in detail in vol. 4, pp. 400–9, of her catalogue.

[23] He also wanted copies of Burney and Arteaga in the University of Virginia Library; see above, pp. 28–29.

[24] The best article on musical glasses and the glass harmonica is A. Hyatt King, "The Musical Glasses and Glass Harmonica." King quotes liberally from Miss Ford's work. There is a glass harmonica, in excellent condition and playable, in the Musical Instruments Room of the Boston Museum of Fine Arts.

how to choose measures at random and assemble them as a minuet or any other musical form. It is not difficult to picture Jefferson, Martha, and the girls enjoying this musical game.

The list of vocal music, Chapter 36 in the Catalogue of 1783, must also have been compiled when Jefferson began the catalogue. Again the list is neatly written and spaced, and only on the verso of the two pages used. By consulting the complete listing of the present music collection again, one notices that, of the catalogue list, Arne's *Lyric Harmony*, J. C. Bach's *Songs*, Baildon's *The Laurel*, Curtis's *The Jessamine*, Dibdin's *Songs*, Haydn's three cantatas, Heron's *Songs*, and Bremner's *Favorite Songs* were all in the bound volume inscribed "John Wayles" and thus may have come to Jefferson through his wife or his father-in-law's estate. Jefferson no doubt saw *Love in a Village*, *Thomas and Sally*, *The Padlock*, *The Deserter*, and *The Beggar's Opera* in Williamsburg and could easily have bought the scores there or in Philadelphia. This vocal music is all typical of the light, graceful, elegant, and charming selections that were popular in England and thus came to be so in America. Most amateurs could sing them at home for enjoyment, as the Jefferson family surely did. Both Hopkinson and Mrs. Cosway wrote their little songs in this genre, but Mrs. Cosway's are, in the tactful words of one writer, "not quite as fortunate musically."[25]

Of the other selections in the chapter devoted to vocal music, only two remain in the Monticello music collection. One of these is the volume containing Handel's *Coronation Anthems* and *Funeral Anthems*, Pergolesi's *Stabat Mater*, and the latter composer's setting of an ode by Alexander Pope. The other surviving item is the Daniel Purcell book of psalms. Interestingly enough, Jefferson did not amend this list by adding the three vocal items we know he acquired in France. He listed *The Beggar's Opera* in his European catalogue (see above, p. 82), but did not check it off in his 1783 catalogue nor did he add Hopkinson's and Mrs. Cosway's songs to it. The latter survive in the present Monticello music collection.

Chapter 37, Jefferson's chapter on instrumental music, shows the most revision and thus is the most difficult to try to read. The verso of the first leaf of this chapter is quite confusing. The handwriting is the same neat, clear script of the previous chapters, but the items are much more compressed on the page. The reader's first thought is that perhaps he added items later, interpolating them between the original lines. However, he cannot have done it much later because the

[25] Nolan, p. 89. Chapters 2 and 3 of Mrs. Nolan's thesis contain an excellent musicological analysis of part 1 of the Jefferson music collection. Parts 2, 3, 4, and 5 were not available to her at the time she wrote her thesis.

entire page is all in the same color ink. Another confusing aspect of this leaf is that many of the items appear to have either faded or been deliberately erased, although the condition of the paper does not support the latter idea. As far as I can determine, Jefferson could have bought all of this music in the United States before 1783. The verso of the second leaf presents no particular problem having again the neat handwriting and even spacing. He lists a second copy of *Love in a Village*, bound with Arnold's sonatas for the harpsichord. He already had a copy of this ballad opera with his vocal music; perhaps he lost it and wanted another one, or perhaps the second one was, as the listing indicates, an instrumental arrangement. Nowhere did he give a complete and detailed listing of the "minuets, country dances, and several books."

On the recto of the second leaf of the instrumental section, Jefferson made a chart categorizing his instrumental music. Since the chart is in black ink and a less regular handwriting, he must have made it later than the original listings. This assumption is supported by the fact that the chart includes the Pugnani opus 10, the Paris edition of the Campioni opus 1, the London edition of the Campioni opus 6 and several compositions by Pleyel, all of which he listed in the catalogue of European purchases. The remaining item in the European catalogue, the Pugnani opus 3, is listed by itself on the recto of the leaf at the end of the instrumental section. In the chart Jefferson listed as "Valentine" the keyboard and violin composer Valentin Nicolai (also spelled Niccolai, or Nicolay). He also listed separately the works of Carlo Antonio Campioni and itemized them more completely than anything else on the page. These facts, plus a music manuscript fragment in Jefferson's handwriting, indicate that Campioni must have been one of his favorite composers.[26]

It is difficult to ascertain just why Jefferson made the chart. Was it supposed to be an acquisition list or a plan for cataloguing what he already possessed? Neither alternative seems to fit. For one thing, on this chart he did not consistently follow his normal practice of making checkmarks to indicate what he owned; only Campioni got a checkmark. Secondly, there are too many omissions. If this is supposed to be a list of what he had, he left out several items of Corelli's, and several of the duet arrangements, all of which his catalogue indicates that he had by 1783 and all of which he could have purchased

[26] Carlo Antonio Campioni (1720–1793) was an Italian composer of chamber music, whose works were very well known in England and America and were available in both countries. As Campioni's works were advertised in the *Virginia Gazette* (Aug. 29, 1771, and Sept. 17, 1772), Jefferson could easily have bought some of them in Williamsburg. Nolan, p. 92.

in Williamsburg or Philadelphia. It is curious also that the chart contains several items, such as the Haydn sonatas and works by Just, Kammel, Agrel, Lampugnani, Martini, Kelly, and Valentin Nicolai that are not listed elsewhere in the catalogue. That is further proof that Jefferson added the chart later than 1783. The whole problem of interpreting the instrumental chapter of the catalogue is further complicated by the fact that account book entries do not coincide with the amount of music we are certain he purchased in Europe or with music we think he might have purchased in Europe.

Further comparison of the instrumental chapter of Jefferson's Catalogue of 1783 with the music in the present Monticello music collection shows even more inconsistancies. The only item in the catalogue exactly describing a volume in the present collection is on the verso of the last leaf in the instrumental section; it is the volume containing works for violin by Corelli, Vivaldi, Tessarini, Wodizka, and Campioni and Chabran. Copies of Bremner's *The Harpsichord or Spinnet Miscellany* and Abel's *Six Favorite Overtures Adapted for the Harpsichord or Organ* (both listed on the last verso of the instrumental section) are also in the present collection, but they are not bound as listed by Jefferson. His copies of Bremner and Abel were in a volume containing Hardin's *Lessons for the Harpsichord* and *Periodical Overtures for the Harpsichord*. In the extant volume, Bremner and Abel are bound with C. P. E. Bach's *Six Sonatas for the Piano-Forte or Harpsichord*, Pergolesi's *Eight Lessons for the Harpsichord* and Snow's *Variations for the Harpsichord*, none of which are in the catalogue at all, although their publication dates indicate that Jefferson could have bought them before he went to France. It is possible that the Bremner and Abel volumes were rebound at a later date with the C. P. E. Bach, Pergolesi, and Snow.

It is also curious that there are so many instrumental works that were obviously bought in Europe and yet are not in either catalogue. Many of these are keyboard selections in which one or more other instruments could participate and thus could have been bought for Patsy as well as for her father. Among these are works by Boccherini, Edelman, Eichner, Mozart, Pleyel, Sterkel, Vento, Gros, Nicolai, Kloffler, Manfredini, Clementi, and Schobert. The Vento, Nicolai, and Schobert items are all French editions published in 1785 and thus were probably bought in France. The Sterkel is a London edition of 1790 and thus could have been bought much later in the United States.

The most recent part of Jefferson's music library to emerge from some forgotten cranny of an attic is a small collection of mostly vocal music, which the Thomas Jefferson Memorial Association acquired late in 1971. It is itemized as Part 5 of Appendix II. The collection consists mostly of sheet music of the 1790s and early 1800s, and probably belonged to the girls, although it is the kind of thing Jefferson himself preferred as he got older. There are some rather interesting things to notice about it. Several of the songs are much older than the publication dates of these editions, indicating that perhaps they were old favorites of the family, purchased, copied, and recopied. "Water Parted From the Sea," for instance, goes farther back than the 1797–98 date of this edition would indicate. Ballad opera and musical farce are represented by selections from Stephen Storace's *My Grandmother* and *The Pirates*, Thomas Attwood's *The Prisoner*, William Reeve's *The Purse* and Samuel Arnold's *The Children in the Wood*. This music was printed in the *Gentleman's Amusement* for May 1, 1796, and the family evidently liked the pieces well enough to tear them out of the magazine and keep them in one of their piles of sheet music.[27] A little book of treble clef melodies might have been used by Jefferson after his bad wrist became too stiff for Corelli, or perhaps the young flageolet players used it. Perhaps Jefferson's grandson Lewis used it, whether playing his grandfather's kit or Browse Trist's flageolet (see above, pp. 44, 47, 40). There is a fragment of a book of Scotch songs of the kind Jefferson liked in later years. There are also some remnants of what must have been some of Patsy's French vocal music—a book of songs from French operas, and four separate sheets of the same, torn from issues of a weekly musical journal published in Paris in the 1780s. One of these songs is "Jour heureux" from *Dardanus*.

One hopes that many more bits and pieces of the Jefferson family music come to light among the possessions of descendants and family friends. It is hard to believe that one lady's servant could have burned the major part of such a large music library, or that most of the library even went to one person. The discovery and proper safekeeping of more of the Jefferson family music would furnish interesting and valuable information about both the man and the time in which he lived.

[27] According to the Music Division, DLC, the sheet numbered pp. 53–54 may be the only extant copy of that particular page of the May 1, 1796, issue of the *Gentleman's Amusement*. See p. 123.

Conclusions

THE USUAL REACTION to learning of Thomas Jefferson's musical pursuits is "Oh, did he do that, too? Was he any good?" While no one can really prove whether or not he was "any good," it is nevertheless possible to draw some conclusions about his musical life: his probable skill as a performer; whether the mechanical aspect of music was more interesting to him than the aesthetic; and some general observations about the place he assigned to music among the many and varied interests of his life.

A sufficient number of persons refer to Jefferson's violin playing to enable us to assume that he was probably a fairly proficient, better-than-average gentleman amateur violinist. As a young law student, he was sufficiently advanced to be asked to join Governor Fauquier's musical evenings, where tradition says he played second violin. Jefferson told Nicholas Trist that he took violin lessons from Francis Alberti, probably during the years of his marriage, and that while he was taking lessons he practiced "no less than 3 hours a day."[1] The German and English officers who lived near Monticello after the Battle of Saratoga all thought highly of his violin playing—one of them said that Jefferson was the best amateur violinist he had ever heard.[2] François-Jean, Marquis de Chastellux, who visited Monticello in 1782, left one of the most perceptive descriptions of Jefferson's mind and talents, naming him a musician and a man of many talents.[3] Another friend said that he played the cello "passably."[4] The only adverse word comes from an author who says that "grand-

[1] Trist, Memorandum. No doubt he practiced faithfully, but it is wise to remember that this was an old man recalling events of fifty to sixty years before and that amateur musicians frequently exaggerate when telling others how much they practice.

[2] Morgan Dix, comp., *Memoirs of John Adams Dix* (New York, 1833), I, 59.

[3] Marquis de Chastellux, *Travels in North America* (London, 1787), II, 42ff.

[4] H. R. Marraro, ed., *Memoirs of the Life of Philip Mazzei* (New York, 1942), p. 226.

mothers in Virginia, who heard the truth from the preceding generation . . . quote an early authority as saying that Patrick Henry was the worst fiddler in the colony, with the exception of Thomas Jefferson."[5]

Although Jefferson told Nicholas Trist that he "laid aside" his violin when the Revolution began and never took it up again,[6] we know that he continued buying violin strings and music up into the 1790s. Perhaps he meant that after the Revolution he never studied seriously again, but continued to play for recreation and enjoyment and of course to play duets with Patsy and the girls to encourage their keyboard studies. The slave Isaac said that his master played the violin in the parlor at Monticello in the afternoons and sometimes after supper. "This was in his early time. When he begin to git so old, he didn't play."[7] An unidentified former student at the University of Virginia told an interviewer that Jefferson took great pleasure in performing on the violin, even in extreme old age. A Charlottesville resident rather vaguely connected to the staff of Monticello told the same interviewer that Jefferson was a very good violinist, but that he never played for very long at a time.[8] Jefferson's last recorded purchase of violin strings was late in 1792 in Philadelphia,[9] but that does not necessarily mean that he never again bought any. It is most likely that the combination of the presidential work load, and his bad wrist caused him to play less frequently after the 1790s.

There has always been a tradition that Jefferson played the violin frequently for his grandchildren and their friends to dance to, after he retired permanently to Monticello. This probably comes from reminiscences of his grandson, Thomas Jefferson Randolph, who wrote that "Before he lost his taste for the violin, in winter evenings, he would play on it, having his grandchildren dancing around him."[10] By the time the granddaughters were old enough to invite friends and cousins for evening dancing at Monticello, Jefferson was obviously not playing the violin on such occasions. In their letters the

[5] William E. Curtis, *The True Thomas Jefferson* (Philadelphia, 1901), pp. 24–25. The "early authority" and his qualifications as a critic are not given. If he was only used to country fiddling, his ear was accustomed to the modal scales, to the absence of vibrato, and to notes and rhythm rather than tone quality. Art music such as Jefferson played would have sounded out of tune to him. Cyclone Covey, p. 546.

[6] Trist, Memorandum.

[7] Isaac Jefferson, p. 13.

[8] Daniel, pp. 1766, 1768.

[9] Account Books, Dec. 24, 1792.

[10] Thomas Jefferson Randolph, quoted in Randall, III, appendix 36.

granddaughters spoke of many evenings of dancing at Monticello, but only to the music of the old harpsichord or a Negro fiddler (see above, p. 40).

Nicholas Trist, who courted Virginia in person and by correspondence for six years before marrying her in 1824, never mentioned having heard her grandfather play the violin. Neither Nicholas nor Virginia ever referred to Jefferson's violins, or his violin playing, during the two years they lived with him at Monticello after their marriage. Nicholas's memorandum of March 22, 1826, indicates that he knew very little about Jefferson's violins, and, out of curiosity, asked him about them. If Nicholas, who spent so much time at Monticello, knew next to nothing about the violins and never spoke of having heard his grandfather-in-law play them, one can assume that the old man did not play much during the last few years of his life.

When Joseph Coolidge received Jefferson's violins to sell, he said that they were not in playable condition and indicated that no one had used them for a long time. He did not, however, speak of any specific damage to them; he noted only that they had no strings or bridges. He did not say whether or not the "celebrated performer," whom he persuaded to examine the violins, tried to play them as part of his examination. If they really were unplayable, Jefferson probably had not played them for several years. On the other hand, if they were much more badly damaged than Coolidge indicated, he could not have expected to sell them advantageously in England and certainly would not have bothered to send them there.

Perhaps the best evaluation of Jefferson's ability as a violinist comes from his granddaughter Ellen Wayles Randolph Coolidge. This intelligent and witty lady idolized her "dear grandpapa," but she shows balanced judgment about his violin playing in her notebook of comments on Henry S. Randall's biography of Jefferson:

> With regard to Mr. Jefferson's skill on the violin. . . . Mr. Randall's idea that he became "one of the best violinists of his day" is a little extreme. My grandfather would, I believe, have disclaimed it. When we remember that the violin is a most difficult instrument, and that great proficiency in the management of it requires the labor of a life—that sixteen hours out of twenty-four have sometimes been devoted to it, we see at once that the time given to music by Mr. Jefferson could never have accomplished more than a gentlemanly proficiency. No amateur violinist could hope to equal a professor. Mr. Jefferson played I believe very well indeed, but not so well as to stand a comparison with many other persons especially such as he must have met with abroad.[11]

[11] Ellen Randolph Coolidge, Manuscript notebook of comments on H. S. Randall's biography of TJ, pp. 36–37, EWC, ViU.

In expressing so much interest in the mechanical aspects of music, Jefferson reflects the spirit of the age in which he lived. What could be more typical of a man of the Age of Reason than the fact that he was interested in the technical side of his "delightful recreation"? And he was a good technician as his descriptions and discussions of the celestina, the "portable grand," and the quilling of harpsichords attest. Oddly enough, this violinist does not display the depth of technical knowledge of violins that he does of keyboard instruments, but on the other hand a violin does not have so many fascinating and intricate working parts.

Before categorizing Jefferson as a mere musical mechanic, one must remember that he and his contemporaries regarded the gadgets that interested him as legitimate attempts to make musical instruments more versatile. Today we read descriptions of celestinas and Merlin's "forte piano stop" with a smile. However, Jefferson, Hopkinson, Burney, and others were really trying to do things that would make keyboard instruments sound as well as work better. Jefferson described the celestina the way a very good mechanic would, but only a mechanic who appreciated the effect of the celestina could distinguish between the plucked- and bowed-string effects and know what music his daughter should use for it. The same holds true for his other mechanical abilities. He tuned, strung, and restored keyboard instruments so that, musically, they would be enjoyable to listen to. And we know that, after he ceased to exchange letters full of technical details with friends, he continued to take an active interest in what and how well his girls played, and whether or not they had adequate instruments to play on. He also wanted music instruction available to students at the university.

Thomas Jefferson made such scanty comments about music in the vast amount of his writings that it is difficult to determine just exactly what place he assigned it among the many interests that occupied his amazingly versatile mind. It appears, however, that, even though he did not say much about music, he surrounded himself with it and maintained a constant and lively interest in it.

At one period of his life, he described American music somewhat unjustly as being in a state of "deplorable barbarism," and in the same letter he expressed the wish that he could import from Europe persons who could supply his domestic needs and in addition form a little domestic orchestra:

I retain for instance . . . a gardiner . . . weaver . . . a cabinet maker . . . and a stonecutter . . . to which I would add a Vigneron. In a country where, like yours, music is cultivated and practiced by every class of men I suppose there might be found persons of those trades who could perform on the French horn, clarinet or hautboy and bassoon, so that one might have a band of two French horns, two clarinets and hautboys and a bassoon.[12]

A few years later he expressed himself in a way that embraced more than merely a wish to have his own little orchestra:

You see that I am an enthusiast on the subject of the arts. But it is an enthusiasm of which I am not ashamed, as its object is to improve the taste of my countrymen, to increase their reputation, to reconcile to them the respect of the world and procure them its praise.[13]

Nevertheless, he did not personally do anything to improve American music—he was much too busy with other things and he certainly never had any extra money to patronize musicians.

Thomas Jefferson seldom said anything about what he thought of composers and performers. He barely acknowledged receiving compositions of his friends, Hopkinson and Mrs. Cosway. The only composer for whom he left some record of preference was Carlo Antonio Campioni. He carefully copied down themes of Campioni's works that he already had, then noted: "On this paper is noted the beginning of the several compositions of Campioni which are in possession of T. Jefferson, he would be glad to have everything else he has composed of Solos, Duets, or Trios, printed copies would be preferred, but if not to be had, he would have them in manuscript.[14] His granddaughter, Ellen Coolidge, said that he was particularly fond of sacred music, especially the old psalm tunes, and that throughout the time she knew him he constantly sang or hummed psalm tunes, Scotch songs, and occasionally Italian airs.[15] As to performances, Jefferson told Trist that he heard Viotti often in Paris, but "never derived the same pleasure from him that I have from [Francis] Alberti."[16] One must remember, however, that this was the remark of an old man associating Alberti's playing with the happiest period of his life.

It is interesting to observe that this man, who was surrounded by black people, seemed not the least bit curious about or interested in their music. He referred to black music in only one place in his works, stating that he believed black people to be gifted with accurate ears for tune and time, and perhaps capable of imagining short

[12] TJ, Williamsburg, to Giovanni Fabbroni, June 8, 1778, Boyd II, 196.
[13] TJ to James Madison, Sept. 20, 1785, Boyd VIII, 535.
[14] Item #34, Monticello music collection, ViU. The item is undated.
[15] Ellen Coolidge, comments on Randall's biography of TJ, pp. 14, 34.
[16] Trist, Memorandum.

melodies, but he doubted that they could handle the more sophisticated aspects of composition and harmony. He mentioned that they played the "Banjar," which they brought from Africa.[17]

Jefferson's music library remains today the best evidence for his "most decided taste for music and great natural disposition for it."[18] It is the library of a man who obviously did enjoy participating in and listening to all kinds of music, even if he did not make profound statements about it. He did not philosophize about music, or speculate upon its position among the arts; he did not intend to. Although he once referred to music as a "favorite passion" of his soul, it was never really as favorite a passion with him as architecture, gardening, and his many other interests. He simply enjoyed his music both aesthetically and technically. It was his "resource . . . against ennui,"[19] the "companion which will sweeten many hours,"[20] and above all, it was his "delightful recreation."

[17] TJ, *Notes on the State of Virginia* (New York, 1964), p. 135.

[18] Ellen Coolidge, p. 37.

[19] TJ to Robert Skipwith, Aug. 3, 1771, Boyd I, 78.

[20] TJ to Martha Jefferson Randolph, Apr. 4, 1790, Betts and Bear, *Family Letters*, p. 51.

Appendixes

Glossary

Bibliography

Index

APPENDIX I:

Jefferson's Catalogue of 1783
*Transcription of the Music Section**

5. Music. Chap. 35. Theory.

√Holden's essay towards a rational system of music.
√Jackson's scheme of sounds with the preliminary discourse.
The same.
√Bremner's rudiments of music. $12^{mo.}$
√Burney's present state of music in Italy . $8^{vo.}$
√Burney's present state of music in Germany . $8^{vo.}$
Burney's history of music.
√Geminiani's art of playing the violin } in 1 vol. fol.
√__________ rules for playing in taste }
√Heck's art of playing the harpsichord
√Compleat tutor for the harpsichord.
√Pasquali's art of fingering the harpsichord. }
√Pasquali's Thorough bass made easy - - - - - } in 1. vol. fol.
√Zuccari's method of playing Adagios }
Miss Ford's instructions for playing on the musical glasses.
√Compleat tutor for the German flute.
√Hoegi's tabular system of minuets.

* Transcription from Nolan, pp. 112–19.

Rivoluzioni del teatro musicale Italiano. dal Arteaga. 3 v. 8$^{vo.}$

Chap. 36 Vocal

√La buona figliuola del Piccini
Alfred, a masque
Artaxerxes
√Love in a Village
√Thomas and Sally
√The Padlock
√The Deserter
The Beggar's Opera
√Handel's Alexander's feast, the words by Dryden
√Handel's Coronation anthems }
√Handel's Funeral anthems } in score 1 vol.
√Stabat mater by Pergolesi }
√Pope's ode by the same }
Henry Purcell's Harmonia sacra. 2.v.
√Daniel Purcell's psalms set for the organ.
Playford's book of psalms
Purcell's 50 psalms set to Music
The [?] companion, a collection of hymns and anthems.
Butt's miscellany of sacred music.
√Purcell's Orpheus Britannicus. fol.
√The same.
Howard. British Orpheus. 6 books
√Clio & Euterpe. 3. v. 8vo.
√Arne's Lyric harmony, op. 4 th.
Arne's Select English songs, 9 books.
√Baildon's Laurel 2d book.
√Hayden's Cantatas.
Pasquali's songs.
Jackson's songs.

36.

√Drinking songs. 2 books
√Curtis's Jessamine
√Bach's songs 2d collection
√Heron's songs books 4th & 5th
√Favorite songs published by Bremner
√Dibdon's songs 8vo
√book of songs 8vo
√Book of songs folio.

Chapt. 37 Instrumental

√Corelli's concertos in parts.
√Vivaldi's concertos in parts.
√12 Concertos chosen from the works of Vivaldi. 1st part.
Vivaldi's Cuckoo & Extravaganza
Hasse's grand Concerto
Pergolesi's Overtures
√Handel's 60 overtures from all his Operas and Oratorios, 8 parts
√E. of Kelly's Overtures in 8 parts, Op. 1 (2d violin wanting)
√Arne's Charke's Lampe's medley overtures in parts
√Abel's overtures in 8 parts, op. 1
√Howard's Overtures in the Amorous goddess in parts.
√Corelli's. Sonatas. 4 operas by Cooke. 4 parts.
√Corelli's Sonatas op. 7th
√Lampugnani's Sonatas op. 1 } in 3 parts. 3 vols.
√Corelli's Sonatas. 4 operas
√Pasquali's 12 Sonatas in 2 sets } in 4 vols.
√Humphries' Sonatas
√Corelli's 6 Sonatas, Op. 3
√ √ √
√Martini of Milan's Sonatas. Op. 1.2.3.4.
√Abel Overtures Op. 1 in 3 parts
√Lampugnani's Sonatas.
√Giardini's 6 trios, op. 17.
√ √ √ √
√Campioni's Sonatas Op. 1.2.3.4.5.6.7.
√Humble's Sonatas
√ √
√Boccherini's Sonatas op. 2.11.
√Gasparini's Sonatas.
√M.S. Sonatas by Kammel, Vanhall, & Schwindel
√Campioni's 6. duets.
√Roeser's 6 duets, op. 2
√Godwin's 6 duets.
√Tessarini's duets, op. 2
√Bezossi's duets.
√ √ √
√Martini of Milan's duets op. 4.7.10.
√Battino's duets
√Figlio's nocturnes } in 2 vols. folio.
√Figlio's duets
√Campioni's duets op. 8
√ √
√Degiardino's duets op. 2. 13.

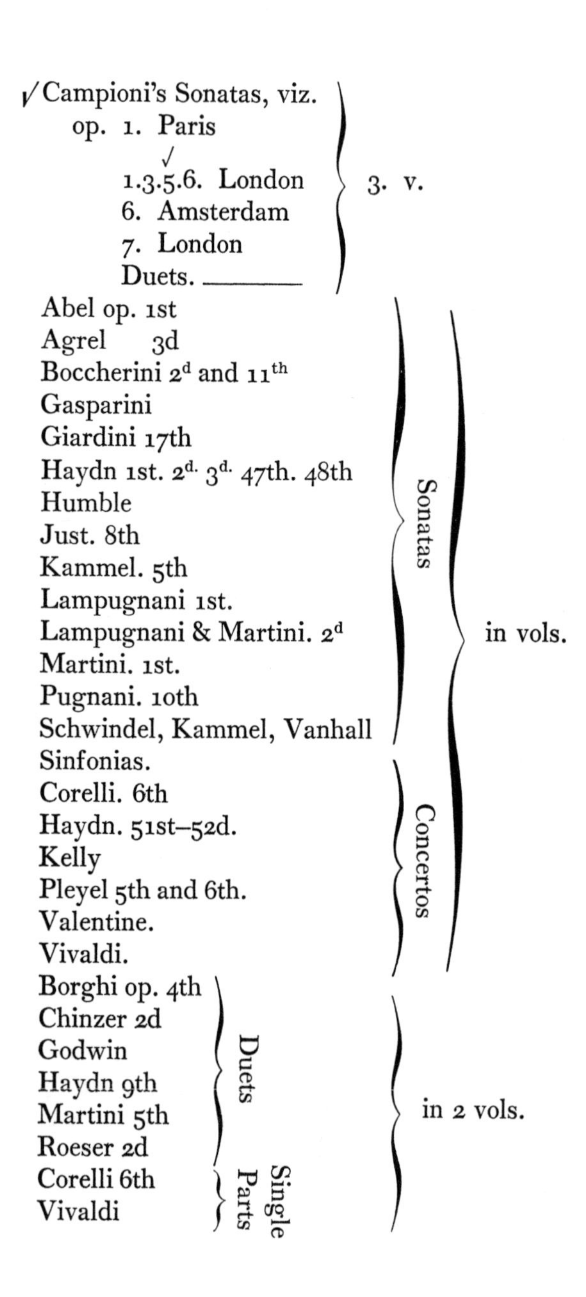

√ Campioni's Sonatas, viz.
op. 1. Paris
√ 1.3.5.6. London
6. Amsterdam
7. London
Duets. ———
} 3. v.

Abel op. 1st
Agrel 3d
Boccherini 2d and 11th
Gasparini
Giardini 17th
Haydn 1st. 2d. 3d. 47th. 48th
Humble
Just. 8th
Kammel. 5th
Lampugnani 1st.
Lampugnani & Martini. 2d
Martini. 1st.
Pugnani. 10th
Schwindel, Kammel, Vanhall
} Sonatas

Sinfonias.
Corelli. 6th
Haydn. 51st–52d.
Kelly
Pleyel 5th and 6th.
Valentine.
Vivaldi.
} Concertos

} in vols.

Borghi op. 4th
Chinzer 2d
Godwin
Haydn 9th
Martini 5th
Roeser 2d
} Duets

Corelli 6th
Vivaldi
} Single Parts

} in 2 vols.

37.

√Corelli's Solos by Cooke.

√Corelli's Solos, op. 5
√Vivaldi's Solos, op. 2
√Tessarini's solos, op. 2
√Wodizka's solos.
√Campioni's & Chabran's solos.
} 1 vol. fol.

√Geminiani's 12. solos, op. 1 – – – – – –
√Degiardino's 12. sols.
√Degiardino's 6. harpsichord sonatas, op. 3
} 1 vol. fol.

√Burgess's lessons for the harpsichord.
√Boccherini's Sonatas for the harpsichord.
√Felton's Concertos, op. 1
√Stamitz's concertos for the harpsichord
} 1 vol. fol.

√Bremner's harpsichord miscellany
√Hardin's lessons for the harpsichord.
√Abel's Overtures
√Periodical Overtures for the harpsichord.
} 1 vol. fol.

√Heron's voluntaries ——————
√Bach's Sonatas Op. 10

√Arnold's Sonatas for the harpsichord.
√Love in a Village
} 1 vol. fol.

Handel's lessons
Lully's lessons.
Felton's lessons.
Stanley's solos.
√Geminiani's minuet
√Minuets, country dances, and several books
√Thumoth's English, Scotch, & Irish airs.
√Thumoth's Scotch and Irish airs.
√Pocket companion for the German flute. 8vo.

Pugnani's Solos, op. 3.

APPENDIX II

Collections of Jefferson Family Music

Part 1

Monticello music collection: Manuscripts Department, Alderman Library, ViU, Acc. No. 3177. When this collection was acquired, it was sorted and stored in six boxes and one oversize box. For convenience, I itemize it according to the manner in which it is presently stored.

Box 1, folder 1:

Minuets with their Basses . . . for German Flute, Violin, or Harpsichord. [London, ca. 1753]. This book contains about 110 short minuets, some with names and some without. Those named are generally named after some person, or simply after the composer.

Box 1, folder 2:

Manuscript music book containing a mixture of songs, hymns, excerpts from Corelli violin solos, minuets, and scales and preludes in all of the major and minor keys. Several hands are represented, and some of the writing has been identified as that of Martha Wayles Jefferson.

Box 1, folder 3:

Several individual pieces of music bound into one volume:

Stabat Mater, composed by Sigr. [Giovanni Battista] Pergolesi. [London, ca. 1749].

An Ode—The Dying Christian to His Soul, by Mr. [Alexander] Pope . . . adapted to the principal airs of the hymn, *Stabat Mater*, composed by Pergolesi. [London, ca. 1764].

The Anthem Which Was Performed in Westminster Abbey at the Funeral of Her most Sacred Majesty, Queen Caroline. Composed by Mr. [Georg Friedrich] Handel. Vol. II. [London, ca. 1770].

Handel's Celebrated Coronation Anthems [three] *in Score, for Voices and Instruments*. Vol. I, [London, 1743].

Box 1, folder 4:

The Psalms Set Full for the Organ or Harpsichord, by Mr. Daniel Purcell, [London, n.d.] Several have the words written in, possibly in Martha Randolph's handwriting.

The book contains: "Canterbury Tune," "York Tune," "Southwell Tune," "St. Mary's Tune," "100th Psalm Tune," "Windsor Tune," "London Tune," "St. David's Tune" (one of TJ's favorites), "119th Psalm Tune," "148th Psalm Tune," "113th Psalm Tune."

Box 1, folder 5 (filed in oversize box):

Songs and Duets composed by Mrs. Cosway. 8 pages of short songs and duets in Italian, with harp accompaniment.
Seven Songs by Francis Hopkinson, [ca. 1784]. Hopkinson dedicated these songs to George Washington. He sent Washington and Jefferson each a copy of them in December, 1788.

Box 1, folder 6:

Volume of several groups of selections, bound together:

The Harpsichord or Spinnet Miscellany . . . by Robert Bremner. [London, ca. 1765].

Six Sonatas for the Piano-Forte or Harpsichord, Composed by Sigr. C. E. [Carl Philip Emanuel] Bach. [Ca. 1775].

Eight Lessons for the Harpsichord, Composed by Giovanni Battista Pergolesi. [London, ca. 1771].

Variations for the Harpsichord to a Minuet of Corelli's, the Gavot in Otho [by Handel], *and the Old Highland Laddie*, by J. Snow. [London, ca. 1769].

Six Favorite Overtures Adapted for the Harpsichord or Organ, Composed by C[hristian] F[erdinand] Abel. [London, ca. 1769–75].

Box 2, folder 7:

Six Concerto [*sic*], *pour le Clavecin ou le Forte-Piano* . . . Composed by J. S. Schroetter. Oeuvre III. [Paris, ca. 1785].
Ouverture et Airs de Ballets D'Alexandre aux Indies, by de Mereaux, arranged for Clavecin or Forte-Piano by the author . . . . [ca. 1765].

Box 2, folder 8:

Green bound volume of manuscript music, entitled *Sonatas Pour le Clavecin par differens auteurs 1788*. Contains:

Pasquali's method of tuning the harpsichord
Sonata—Ferdinand Stoes
Rondeau
Sonata—Ernest Eixner [Eichner]
"The Merman's Song"—Haydn
Overture from *Alexandre Aux Indies* [by de Mereaux]
Duke of York's March
Chorus—des Voyageurs de la Caravanne
"The Shipwrecked Seaman's Ghost"
"Tis Not the Bloom on Damon's Cheek"

There are several much smaller sheets in this volume that are obviously not part of it, but were just placed there. They contain: "Black Eyed Susan," "Two Catches," "War Song"—from Moore, "Dulce Domum," "My Nanie O."

Box 2, folder 9:

Bound volume, with green cover, contains:
Quatre Sonates pour la Harpe . . . by [Valentino] Nicolai
Trois Sonates Pour la Clavecin ou le Piano-Forte . . . by Nicolai
Trois Duos Concertants pour le Clavecin ou Forte-Piano . . . by Nicolai

All of these are typical of the many selections published in arrangements for solo instrument and thoroughbass. The keyboard instrument played the thoroughbass and any instrument could be used for the solo—usually the violin or flute was used. These selections by Nicolai were published in France, ca. 1780–83.

In this folder there is also an additional folder of loose pieces of manuscript music and a printed song from Handel's *Alexander's Feast*. They were removed from the collection a number of years ago, and the person who removed them did not know exactly where to put them back.

Box 2, folder 10:

Bound volume, with green cover, contains:
Sei Sonate de Cembalo e Violino Obligato da Luigi Boccherini, Opera V, [Paris, ca. 1780].
Six Sonates pour le Clavecin avec Accompagnement d'un Violon ad Libitum par Mr. [Johann Friedrich] Edelman, Oeuvre I, [Paris, ca. 1780].
Trois Sonates en Trio pour le Clavecin . . . violin et violoncello, par Ernesto Eichner, [Paris, ca. 1780].

Box 3, folder 11:

Bound volume, with brown cover, contains:
- *XII Solos for a Violin with a Thorough Bass for the Harpsichord or Violincello*, composed by Arcangelo Corelli, [London, ca. 1740]. Op. 5.
- *XII Solos for a Violin with a Thorough Bass for the Harpsichord or Bass Violin*, Composed by Antonio Vivaldi, [London, ca. 1721]. Op. 2.
- *XII Solos for a German Flute, or Hoboy or a Violin with a Thorough Bass for the Harpsichord or Bass Violin*, composed by Carlo Tessarini, [London, ca. 1736]. Op. 2.
- *Six Solos for a Violin and Bass*, Composed by Wenceslaus Wodizka, [London, ca. 1750]. Op. 1.
- *Six Favorite Solos for a Violin with a Bass for the Violincello and Harpsichord*, Composed by [Carlo Antonio] Campioni and Sigr. Chabran, [London, ca. 1760].

Box 3, folder 12:

Bound volume, with cover missing, contains:
- "Overture" to *Artaxerxes*, by T. A. Arne, [London, ca. 1790].
- *Haydn's Celebrated Overture*—harpsichord or pianoforte
- *Two Grand Sonatas, for the Piano Forte or Harpsichord, with an Accompaniment for the Violin* . . . by Ignace Pleyel, [London, ca. 1790].
- *Three Sonatas for the Piano Forte or Harpsichord* . . . by E[rnesto] Eichner, [London, ca. 1790].

The following are issues of: *Bland's Collection of Sonatas, Lessons, Overtures, Capricios, Divertimentos, &c, &c for the harpsichord or pianoforte without accompaniment, by the Most Esteemed Composers.* This series was published in London, ca. 1790–94

- No. 21, Vol 2:
  - Edelman's Sonata I, Op. 1
  - Vento—Sonata
- No. 22, Vol 2:
  - Edelman's Sonata I, Op. 16
  - Overture to *The Bastile*
  - Edelman's Sonata II, Op. 16
- No. 28, Vol 3:
  - Pleyel's "Cottage Maid"
  - Edelman's Third Sonata, Op. 8
- No. 29, Vol 3:

Edelman's Third Sonata, Op. 16
Martini's Grand Overture to *Henry the Fourth*
No. 38, Vol 1:4:
Gluck's Overture—*Paradie ed Elena*
Edelman's Sonata IV, Op. 16
No. 42, Vol 1:4:
Overture *Oedipe à Colonne*, Arranged by Lachnitth
Eichner's fourth Sonata
Haydn's Grand Orchestra Sinfonie, adapted for Piano Forte or Harpsichord. With an Accompaniment for Violin by Rimbault, [London, ca. 1785].
Haydn's Grand Orchestra Sinfonie . . . at the Nobility's Concerts. Adapted for Organ, Harpsichord, or Piano Forte. [London, ca. 1785.]
Concerto, pour le Clavecin . . . by J. C. Fischer, Berlin and Amsterdam, n.d.

Box 3, folder 13:

Several loose sheets, some unidentifiable:
1. "The Plain Gold Ring," "Buy a Broom," "I'd Be a Butterfly," "Let Us Haste to Kelvin Grove"
2. Overture to *The Deserter*
3. 12 pages of unidentifiable sheets

Box 3, folder 14:

Bound volume, with green cover, contains:
Pieces de Clavecin par M. Balbastre, [Paris, ca. 1765]—a group of 16 short pieces
Trois Quatuors de Mr. Ignace Pleyel . . . , [Paris, ca. 1785]
Trois Sonates pour le Clavecin . . . by Leopold Kozeluch, [Paris, ca. 1788]
Trois Sonates pour Clavecin . . . by J. S. Schroetter, [Paris, ca. 1785]
A Duett for two Performers on One Forte Piano, by Sigr. [Muzio] Clementi, op. VI, [London, ca. 1786].

Box 4, folder 15:

Bound volume, with green cover, contains:
Six Sonatas pour le Clavecin . . . par Jean Cretien Bach [Oeuvre V] [Paris, ca. 1780].

La Chasse pour le Clavecin . . . par Muzio Clementi, Oeuvre XVI, [London, ca. 1786].
Trio pour le Clavecin . . . Violon . . . par W[olfgang] A[madeus] Mozart, Ouevre 16, [ca. 1775, Paris].

Box 4, folder 16:

Manuscript book of songs, waltzes, melodies from operas, tables of note values and rests, and miscellaneous unidentifiable pieces, in several different handwritings. Leaves of music are tied together with string.

Box 4, folder 17:
Unidentifiable printed scraps and fragments, including six sonatas.

Box 4, folder 18:

Trois Quatuors de M. Ignace Pleyel. With Violin accompanyment by [Ludwig Wenzil] Lachnitth, [Paris, ca. 1788].

Box 4, folder 19:

Ouverture de la Bonne Fille . . . arrangee Pour le Clavecin . . . par L. F. Despreaux, [Paris, ca. 1785].

Box 4, folder 20:

A group of selections from some operas popular in Paris during the Jeffersons' stay there: "Le Carillon des Trois Fermiers," "Trio d'Azor," "Air des Trois Fermiers," "Rose Chérie de Zemire et Azor," "Air de Trois Fermiers." There are notes and lyrics throughout the pieces in the handwriting of Martha Jefferson (Randolph).

Box 4, folder 21:

Unbound scrap containing two sonatas, or parts of two sonatas, by Edelman, Op. VII, for pianoforte and violin.

Box 4, folder 22:

Bound volume, with covers missing, contains:
Harpsichord Sonatas by Dibdin
Easy Lessons for Harpsichord . . . by Wagenseil
Three Minuets by Graff, Toeschi and Tenducci
Sonata by Pescetti

Lessons by Giovanni, Rutini, Green, and Castrucci [London, ca. 1770–80]

Box 4, folder 23:

Bound volume, containing three small volumes of French songs, mainly pastorals, romances, and rondos:

Recueil de Petits Airs . . . Darondeau, Oeuvre VI, [Paris, ca. 1785].

Recueil de Romances et D'Ariettes . . . Darondeau, Oeuvre IV, [ca. 1785].

Recueil de Petits Airs de Chant . . . Martini, [ca. 1770].

Box 5, folder 24:

Large bound volume, with MISS JEFFERSON [*sic*] stamped in gold on the cover, contains:

Le Tout—Ensemble, de Musique, pour le Forte Piano, ou Clavecin avec Accompagnemens par les grands Maîtres de L'Europe . . . [ca. 1786]. There are a few fragmentary and unidentifiable selections from this collection. Some of them are violin parts.

Several pages of untitled manuscript music, inscribed "Maria Jefferson" at the beginning.

Niccolai's Opera 3rd, Sonata III, IV, V, VI, [ca. 1785].

Six Sonatas . . . [keyboard and violin] . . . by T. Sterkel, Opera III, [London, ca. 1790].

Sei Sonate . . . [keyboard and violin] . . . Matia Vento, Opera II, [Lyon, ca. 1785].

Quatre Sonates . . . [harp, violin, bass] . . . M. Gros [III omitted] Oeuvre III, [Paris, ca. 1770].

Unidentified sonatas 4, 5, and 6, arranged for piano duet.

Six Sonates . . . [keyboard and violin] . . . Valentin Nicolay, Oeuvre XI, [ca. 1785].

Concertos 1–4, op. XI–XV . . . Schobert [keyboard], [London, ca. 1790].

Sigr. [*Joseph*] *Haydn's Grand Orchestra Sinfonie* [no. 1] *as Performed at the Nobility's Concerts, adapted for the Organ, Harpsichord or Piano Forte*, [London, ca. 1785].

The Celebrated Overture La Chasse . . . Haydn [keyboard], [London, ca. 1785].

A Concerto [no. 3] . . . [keyboard and instruments] . . . J. F. Kloffler, [London, ca. 1780].

A Favorite Concerto . . . [keyboard and instruments] by Vincent Manfredini, [London, n.d.].
The Celebrated Overture [to Sinfonie II] . . . by Haydn [keyboard] [London, ca. 1790].
Three Sonatas [keyboard] . . . by Mozart, [London, ca. 1786].

Box 5, folder 25:

Bound volume, with green cover, contains:
Sonates in Quatuor pour le Clavecin . . . par Mr. Balbastre . . . Oeuvre III, [Paris, ca. 1780].
Six Sonates . . . [keyboard and violin] . . . Mr. [Muzio] Clementi, Oeuvre II, [Paris, ca. 1783].
Six Sonatas for the Piano Forte or the Clavecin . . . by Clementi, Opus IV, [London, ca. 1783].
La Chasse pour Le Clavecin ou Forte Piano par Leopold Kozeluch, Oeuvre V, [Vienne, ca. 1781].

Box 6, folder 26:

Bound volume, with green cover, contains:
Sonates pour le Clavecin . . . Opera V, par M. [Johann] Schobert, [Paris, ca. 1785].
Sonatas en Quatuor pour le Clavecin . . . Schobert, Oeuvre III, [Paris, ca. 1785].
Sinfonies pour le Clavecin . . . Schobert . . . Opera IX, [Paris, ca. 1785].
Sinfonies pour le Violon et Cors de Chasse . . . Schobert, Opera X, [Paris, ca. 1785].
Six Sonates pour Clavecin Ou Forte Piano . . . Jean Cretian Bach, Oeuvre XV, [Paris, ca. 1775–79].

Box 6, folder 27:

Manuscript and music book inscribed "Virginia J. Randolph." Several different handwritings. Contains: Overture to *Lodoiska* by Knetzer; Dutch Minuet; "Murphy Delany"; "Jack Lahn"; Variations to "Duncan Grey"; song by Lord Lytellton; "New Crazy Jane"; "Arietta" from *La Fausse Magie;* "Rural Felicity" with variations.

Box 6, folder 28:

Manuscript music book inscribed "Ellen Wayles Randolph, Eliza Waller, Jane Blair Cary." Several different handwritings and many unidentified pieces. Contains: "La Canonade" by Balbastre; "God Save the Commonwealth"; "Rise Cynthia Rise"; "Lullaby"; Sonata of Edelman; German Waltz.

Box 6, folder 29 (in oversize box):

Many loose sheets of fragmentary manuscripts in various handwritings, a few pieces tied together with string. Contains: "Vedrai Carino"; "New York Serenading Waltz"; "Fin Ch'han del vion" from *Don Giovanni* by Mozart; "Aurora"; "Batti Batti" from *Don Giovanni* by Mozart; "Valse Hongroise"; several vocal exercises; Rondo de Paganini; Air de Ballet; "Charming Village Maid"; "There's Nothing True But Heaven"; Musette D'*Armide*; Air de Danse de *Roland*; Sonata by Haydn; Duo de *Blaise et Babet*; "Ye Lingring Winds."

Box 6, folder 30 (in oversize box):

Manuscript music book, bound but fragmentary, contains: Variations on Sicilian Hymn; "Life Let Us Cherish"; "The Knight Errant"; "The Portrait"; Hungarian Waltz; "Come Rest in This Bosom"; "The Ill Wife"; A Favorite Scots Air; Air in *The Battle of Marengo*; "The Waltz Cotillion"; "Fin Ch'han del Vino"; "De Tanti. Palpiti"; "Merrily Danced the Quaker's Wife"; "Je Suis Lindor"—Air du *Barbier de Seville*; The Spanish Fandango; "The Haunted Tower"; Clementi's Grand Waltz; Overture of *Panurge*—Grétry; Overture de *Chimene*; Choeur de Voyageurs de la Caravanne; Air Lison Dormoit; "Home Sweet Home"; "There's Nae Luck About the House"; vocal scales and exercises; Bonaparte's Grand March; A Much Admired Waltz by Mozart; "God Save the Emperor"; "Lord Courtney"; "Gramachree"—with variations.

Box 6, folder 31:

New and Complete Preceptor for the Spanish Guitar, Philadelphia, publ. by John Klemm, 1827, sold at P. Thompson, Washington. Contains 14 pages, some obviously missing: several pages of instructions and exercises; "Come Rest in This Bosom"; "Where Roses Wild Were Blowing"; "The Gallant Troubadour"; "Comin' Thru the Rye"; "Draw the Sword Scotland."

Box 6, folder 32:

Der Freischutz (opera) by Carl Maria von Weber. Complete score, inscribed on title page, "Margaretta Deverell."

Box 6, folder 33:

Small manuscript music notebook of songs, in handwritings of Martha Jefferson Randolph and several others. Contains: "A Poor Little Gypsy"—by Arne; "The Silver Moon"—by Hook; "Owen," a Welch Song; "Ellen Aroon"; "Flutt'ring Spread Thy Purple Pinions"; Air du *Barbier de Seville*; "Life Let Us Cherish"; "Song in the Stranger"; "Crazy Jane"; "When Pensive I thought of My Love"—from *Bluebeard*; "The Tear"; "Poor Richard"; "Ah! Gentle Hope"; "The Sailor Boy"; "The Wedding Day"; "Dear Nancy I've Sailed the World All Around"; "M'ha Detto la mia mama"—by Martini; "Thou Art Gone Awa' Mary"; "Flora"; "A Prey to Tender Anguish"; "Psalm 148"; "Old 100th Psalm"; "Psalm 134"; "Psalm 57, verse 8" by Handel; "Psalm 146, verse 6" by Handel; "Psalm 42, verse 9" by Handel; "Easter Hymn"; "Sanctus"; "Lewis Gordon"; "Evening Hymn"; "The Mermaids Song," by Haydn; "The Blind Boy"; "Duke of York's March."

Box 6, folder 34:

Two pages of manuscript music and notes in the hand of Thomas Jefferson. Opening phrases of compositions of Carlo Antonio Campioni which Jefferson owned, inscribed "On this paper is noted the beginning of the several compositions of Campioni which are in possession of T. Jefferson. He would be glad to have everything else he has composed of Solos, Duets, or Trios. Printed copies would be preferred; but if not to be had, he would have them in manuscript."

Part 2

Music from the library of Thomas Jefferson. A collection of eighteenth-century songs. Inscribed "John Wayles," father-in-law of Thomas Jefferson. This bound volume is in the Rare Book Room, ViU. It consists of several books of songs and many loose pieces of sheet music all bound together as one volume. In the last part of the volume, many of the loose pieces of sheet music were mounted on pages from the *Bristol Journal*, [ca. 1766–67]. Contents of the volume:

Lyric Harmony—18 entire new ballads, with *Colin and Phaebe* [*sic*] in Score—performed at Vauxhall Gardens by Mrs. Arne and Mr. Lowe—composed by Thomas Augustine Arne—printed—Wm. Smith, Middle Row, Holborn, [ca. 1740–41].

"The Kind Inconstant"
"The Invitation"
"The Charms of Isabel"
"The Complaint"
"The Rover Reclaim'd"
"Philosophy no Remedy for Love"
"Colin's Invitation"
"The Generous Distress'd"
"Kindness and Gracefull Air Preferr'd to Beauty"
"Cloe Generous as Fair"
"The Lovesick Invitation"
"The Fond Appeal"
"To a Lady, who, Being Asked by her Lover for a Token of Her Constancy, Gave Him a Knife"
"The Complaint"
"The Contest Between Love and Glory"
"The Dumps"
"The Happy Bride"
"Colin and Phaebe—a Pastoral"

A Second Collection of Favorite Songs Sung at Vauxhall—composed by J. C. Bach—printed by Welcker in Gerrard St., St. Ann's, Soho, [ca. 1762–68].
"In This Shady Blest Retreat"
"Smiling Venus Goddess Dear"
"Tender Virgins Shun Deceivers"
"Lovely Yet Ungrateful Swain"

The Laurel Book II—English Songs and Cantatas—composed by Mr. Joseph Baildon—printed for I. Walker, in Catherine St. in the Strand, [ca. 1736–66]. Songs listed by first lines.
"Should fate in some kind hour decree"
"Believe not youth with wit or sense to gain the heart of woman"
"Haste, Lorenzo, hither fly" (as Jessica in *The Merchant of Venice*)
"Gentle Youth, ah! why this pressing"
"On pleasure's smooth wings"
"In Cupid's famed school"
"Bid me to live and I will live thy constant swain to be" Cantata

(separate sheet) "The Love Rapture"—by Mr. Arne

The Jessamine collection of songs by Mr. Thomas Curtis, organist of St. Mildred's, Bread St. Printed by I. Cox at Simpson's Musick Shop in Sweeting's Alley, opposite the East Door of the Royal Exchange, [ca. 1765–95].

"The Self Contest"
"The Confused Lover"
"Aminta's Choice"
"Strephon's Invitation"
"The Advice"
"Then Maidens Like Me Resolve to be Free"
"The True Britton"

The Ballads Sung by Mr. Dibdin this Evening at Ranelagh . . . . composed by Mr. Dibdin—printed and sold at the composer's house, at the Lyre and Owl, in St. Martin's Lane; at Mr. Griffin's, bookseller in Catharine St; at Ranelagh House, [ca. 1764–76]. Listed by first lines.

"My Nancy was as neat a jade"
"There was a fair maiden, her name it was Gillian"
(a 22-page "Conclusion Piece"—4-part vocal, also instrumental)

Three Cantatas by Mr. G. Hayden [*Haydn*] printed John Johnson, Harp and Crown in Cheapside, [ca. 1740–62].

"Martillo"
"Thyrsis"
"Neptune and Amymone"

A Collection of Songs Sung at Marybone Gardens—by Mr. Renoldson—music by Mr. Heron, organist of St. Magnus, London Bridge, and to the Earl of Peterborough—Book IV—Longman, Lukey and Co., 26 Cheapside, [ca. 1769–75].

"Young Collin"
"Dolly's Petition"
"Damon and Phyllis"
"The Invitation"
"The Rose"
"The Moth"
"Polly"
"A Hunting Song"

[Same as above] Book V, 1771

"The Cuckoo"

"Damon"
"Stern Winter"
"Rise Glory"
"Patie" (Scotch Song)
"The Choice"

The Favorite Songs Sung At Ranelagh . . . . printed for Robert Bremner, Harp and Hautboy, opposite Somerset House in Strand, [ca. 1762–89].

"Come Ye Hours"—by Vento
"Not on Beauty's Transient pleasure"—by Giardini
"Sylvia"—cantata, the words from Tasso's *Aminta*
"Go, Lovely Rose"—the words taken from Waller's poems
"Phyllis and Silvano"
"Cloris"—from Waller's poems

The following are separate sheets of music, and comprise the last part of the bound volume:

"The Bee"—music by Mr. Collett
"The Adieux—set by Mr. Oswald
"Robin Hood"
"The Maying"
"Bacchus"
"The Fairest of the Fair"
"By My Sighs"
"The Rose"
A New Song—"Come Damon, come, oh haste away"
A Drinking Song sung at Sadler's Wells
"The Banquet"
"Jolly Bacchus"
"The Farmer's Description of London"
"Cupid God of Soft Persuasion"—from *Love in a Village*
"Damon"—set by Mr. Leonard Abingdon
"Volamente, a Rondeau—by Giardini
"The Jolly British Tar"
A Two-Part Song—set by Mr. H. Purcell, "Fill, fill, fill all the Glasses"
"The Mighty Bowl"
Song for Three Voices—Made on the Peace
A Song, with a Trumpet—set by Mr. Henry Purcell, Genius of England
A New Song—"Give us Glasses my Wench"
"Lovely Nancy"—with variations

A Song—"How Wellcome My Shepard"—by Mr. Fischer
Sung by Mr. Prentice at Sadler's Wells—"I'm a Hearty Good Fellow"
Sung by Mr. Jagger at Vauxhall—"In fancy our hopes and fears"
"The Pilgrim"
The Serenade—"My Bliss too long my Bride Denies"—from *The Merchant of Venice*
"Jockey"—favorite new Scotch Ballad (2 copies)
"In Praise of Woman"
"The Second Ode of Anacreon"
"Woman"—set by Mr. J. Soaper
"A Bacchanalian Song"
"Content"—a pastoral
"Time Made Prisoner"
"The Honest Fellow"
"The Ass"
"Push Around the Brisk Glass"
"Platos's Advice"
"The Cottager"
"Delia"—by Dr. Arne
"Still in Hopes to Get the Better of My Stubborn Flame I Try"—Young Meadows' Song in *Love in a Village*
"The Bird"
"May Eve, or Kate of Aberdeen"
"The Full Flowing Bowl"
"The Charms of a Bumper"
"On Friendship"
"This World is a Stage"
"Russell's Triumph"
"The Father Away"—from *Artaxerxes*
"Make Hay Whilst the Sun Shines"
"The Spinning Wheel"
"To Keep My Gentle Jessy"—by Dr. Arne, from *The Merchant of Venice*
"To Some Petty Sinner Go Wheedle and Whine"
"Well, Well, Say No More"—and, "There Was a Jolly Miller"—both from *Love in a Village*
"The Right Thinker"
"When All the Attic Fire was Fled"
"Rule Britannia"—by Dr. Arne
"The Confession"
"Anacreon on Himself"
"The Evening Adventure"

"Nottingham Ale"
The Bacchanalian—"While I quaff the rosy wine"
"Love and Wine in Alliance"
"Whilst I'm Carrouzing"
"Wine, Wine is Alone ye Brisk Fountain of Mirth"
"Woman for Man"
"The New Year's Gift"
"Delia"
"English Ale"
"The Union of Love and Wine"
"Addressed to the Ladies at Ranelegh"
"Sparkling Champaign"
"Ye Fair Married Dames—from *The Way to Keep Him*—by Dr. Arne
"Ye Famed Witty Nine"—sung in Praise of the Half-Moon Society
"Ye Lads and Ye Lasses Who Bloom in Your Prime"
"Ye Mortals that Love Drinking"
"The Triumph of Bacchus"
A Song in Lethe—"Ye Mortals Whom Fancies and Troubles Perplex"
"Bacchus' Invitation"
"Bagnigge Wells"
"Miss Dawson's Hornpipe"
"Jack Latin"

Part 3

Manuscript music book, supposedly belonged to Martha Jefferson Randolph. Several unidentifiable selections and fragments of selections, along with the following listing. Acc. No. 7443–F, Manuscripts Department, ViU.

Sonata du Même
Simphonie del Signor Wonesch
Sonata Del Signor Ernest Eichner
Rondo par Mr. Balbastre
[Italian song]—sung by Sigr. Pacchierotti
Ma Chère Amie—Sigr. Hook
The Mansion of Peace
[Italian song]—del Signor Mortellari
Airs Variés par Mr. Charpentier, Organiste
Aria Matinore Musette
Aria Triste Raison

La Petitte Poste de Paris
Menuet de Fischer
Air des Amours D'Eté
Les Folies D'Espagnes Variées
Ouverture La Buona Figliuola
La Triomphante—sonata
Ouverture de Chimene
Ballet de Chimene
Choeur des Voyageurs—de la Caravanne
Rondeau par J. B. Krumpholtz
Ouverture D'Iphigenie en Aulide
Symphonie del Signor Krumpholtz
March Querrier par Mr. Balbastre
La Canonade du Même
Symphonie du Même
La De Villiers Du Même
Sonata del Signor Scarlati
Les Sauvages—by Mr. Rameau
"In This Still Retirement," and "Let Not Age Thy Bloom Ensnare,"—by Mr. Haydn
Pleyel's Celebrated Quartette from his 5th suite called Le Tout Ensemble
Pleyel's German Hymn with Variations—"Children of the Heavenly King"
"Adeste Fideles"
Duetto del Signor Vicenzo Martini

Part 4

Music manuscript notebook (ca. 1770). This notebook allegedly belonged to Martha Wayles Skelton Jefferson. It contains words and music of several songs. Deposited with Manuscripts Department, ViU, by Mr. James A. Bear, Jr., Curator of Monticello.

Minuet—Mr. Clarke
Camilla
Almaine—Mr. Clarke
"Celia has a thousand charms"
Arietta Bononcini—for Camilla
Aurelia Singing . . . by Mr. Clarke
"The Silver Swans"—by Mr. Jeremiah Clarke
"Love and Folly"

"Fate has decried us"
"Boast No More, Fond Love"
Corant
Epithalamium. . . "Once Cloris Did Fly Me. . ."
A Ground
Symphony
Grave
"Hither, hither, gentle shepherd"
"If You In Love Such Tickling Joys"
"My Song Shall Be Always of the Loving Kindness of the Lord"
Ground by Corelli [Sonata, op. 5, no. 12, Follia con variaziones]
The Ponjury Song—in *Indian Queen*
A Song—Mr. Purcell
A Song in *The Tempest*—Mr. Purcell
An Italian Song
The Chorus in *The Fairy Queen*
Chorus in *The Prophetess*

Part 5

Monticello music collection, Curator's Office, Monticello Acc. No. 71–6331

Folder A

Collection of sheets of music, tied together with string. Some of the pieces are individual editions of songs in sheet music form; a few are selections cut from other volumes. Inscribed "Elizabeth Virginia Lightfoot" and "Elizabeth Virginia Nicholas" in several places. Most of these pieces of music date from the 1790s. There is no way of telling how or when they came into the possession of the Jefferson family. The following list contains as much information on each piece of music in this folder as is available.

"The Caledonian Laddy." Printed by Benjamin Carr and sold at his musical repositories in Philadelphia and New York, and by I. Carr in Baltimore. This edition represents pp. 2–3 in "The favorite songs," by Mr. Hook, published in Philadelphia, [ca. 1794–95].

"Pauvre Jaque." Also printed for Carr, [ca. 1796]. Song with pianoforte accompaniment, French and English words. Below the title is printed, "NB The small notes with the tails downwards must be sung to the French words." This copy is rather washed out, and somebody has gone over parts of it with ink, to make the printing clearer. Sonneck (p. 327) gives Madame B. de Travanet as the composer.

"Ma Belle Coquette." Song with pianoforte accompaniment, by Mr. Hook. Printed for G. Willig, 165 Market St., Philadelphia, [ca. 1795–97].

"Here's the Pretty Girl I Love." Song with pianoforte accompaniment, composed by Mr. Hooke. Printed for J. Hewitt's musical repository, 131 William St., New York; Published, Jan., 1798.

"Negro Philosophy." Song, with Pianoforte accompaniment, written, composed, and sung by Mr. Dibdin in his new entertainment, called the "General Election." Printed and sold at Hewitt's and Carr's. About a third of the second page has been cut off.

"The Confession." A favorite canzonet with an accompaniment for harp or pianoforte, the music by an amateur. French words penciled in, part of last page missing. Printed by Longman and Broderip, 26 Cheapside and 13 Haymarket, London.

"The Sailor's Journal." Song with Pianoforte accompaniment, by Dibdin. Also titled "Nancy" or "Nancy, or the Sailor's Journal." Printed for Carr's, 1797.

"Meg of Wapping." Another selection from Dibdin's "General Election." Pianoforte accompaniment to song, last part of second page missing. Printed for Hewitt's and Carr's, published Dec. 1797–Jan. 1798.

"The Patent Coffin." Song with pianoforte accompaniment, by Mr. Dibdin. Printed for Hewitt's and Carr's, 1797. Page 2 missing.

"Sweet Nan of Hampton Green." Published by G. Willig, Philadelphia, n.d. Song with pianoforte accompaniment, guitar part on second page. Sonneck gives Hook as the composer and 1792–93 as the publication date. This edition is a separate issue.

"Fair Aurora." A "celebrated duett" in Artaxerxes, by Dr. Arne. Duet arrangement, pianoforte accompaniment with figured bass. Published by Mr. Trisobio [Filippo Trisobio, 66 North Front St., Philadelphia, 1796–98].

"Did Not Tyrant Custom Guide Me." Song by Giordani, published by Trisobio (see above). This is a rather peculiar-looking edition, having the voice part written on the second of the three staves.]

*"Within a Mile of Edinbourgh." Song with pianoforte accompa-

niment from Stephen Storace's musical farce, *My Grandmother*, performed at the New Theater, Philadelphia, April 27, 1795.

*"Ever Remember Me." From Storace's opera, *The Pirates*. Melody only (treble cleff), with text in 3 verses.

*"The Drummer" (1st line: "How charming a camp is. . ."). From the opera, *The Prisoner*, by Thomas Attwood. Melody only (treble clef), with text. Begins in the middle of p. 56; p. 57 is missing.

*Unidentified; perhaps last 3 lines of "How Sweet When the Silver Moon" from *The Purse* or *The Benevolent Tar* by William Reeve. Page 53 of above.

*"The Delights of Wedded Love" (1st line: "Mark, my Alford all the joys"). Written and sung by Mrs. Melmoth in Samuel Arnold's opera, *The Children in the Wood*. Performed, Jan. 2, 1795, New York. This copy is the bottom half of p. 53 of above.

*"Say How Can Words a Passion Feign." Song from *My Grandmother*, see above, p. 54.

*"Favorite Country Dance Compos'd by Dibdin." Two treble clef staves only, p. 54 of above.

"The Happy Dreamer." Song with pianoforte accompaniment. No author or composer indicated. Printed and sold by G. Willig, 185 Market St., Philadelphia, [ca. 1798–1804].

"Water Parted From the Sea." Song with pianoforte accompaniment, by Dr. Arne, from *Artaxerxes*, "and adorned with Italian graces by Mr. Trisobio." [Filippo Trisobio, 66 N. Front St., Philadelphia, 1796–98].

"In My Pleasant Native Plains." Song with pianoforte accompaniment. From *The Carnival of Venice*, by Thomas Linley, Sr. Performed in Philadelphia, 1796–97, and in New York, 1798. This song printed and sold by G. Willig, 185 Market St., Philadelphia, [ca. 1798–1804].

"No More His Fears Alarming." Song with pianoforte accompaniment. From Stephen Storace's opera, *The Pirates*. Published by G. Willig, 165 Market St., Philadelphia, [ca. 1795–97].

*These selections are pp. 55–56 and 53–54 from No. 7 of the *Gentleman's Amusement*, published ca. May 1796. According to the Music Division, DLC, this copy of pp. 53–54 is the only extant copy of this page. See Oscar G. Sonneck, *A Bibliography of Early Secular American Music*. Revised and enlarged by William Treat Upton. The Library of Congress, Music Division, 1945. See also correspondence: Mrs. Helen Cripe to Music Division, DLC, from Curator's Office, Monticello, Nov. 10, 1971, and Music Division, DLC, to Mr. Bear and Mrs. Cripe, Nov. 22, 1971.

"Two Bunches a Penny Primroses." Song with pianoforte accompaniment and guitar arrangement. No publisher indicated, [ca. 1800].

"The Rose." Song with pianoforte accompaniment. This copy has no imprint. The song was from *Selima and Azor* by Thomas Linley, Sr. It first appeared in a collection published in Philadelphia in 1789 by Alexander Reinagle, then as a separate piece of sheet music published by Willig, at the 185 Market St. address, [ca. 1798–1804].

Folder B

Pages 17–30 of a collection of songs. All of the pieces in this selection are written in one- or two-staff treble clef arrangements. Arrangements such as this were usually used for violin or flute. None of the songs have lyrics, or any evidence of composers or date of composition and publication. They probably date from the early 19th century. The following tunes are in this collection:

"Oft in the Stilly Night"
"Buy a Broom"
"Wha'll Be King But Charlie"
"Willis Grand March"
"Quick Step"
"I've Been Roaming"
"The Rustic Reel"
"When Thy Bosom Heaves the Sigh"
"Love was Once a Little Boy"
"A Russian Quick Step"
"Blink Over the Burn, My Sweet Laddie"
"The Oracle Waltz"
"Let us Haste to Kelvin Grove"
"Boston Brigade March"
"LaFayettes Quick Step"
"Caspar" from *Der Fryschutz* [*sic*]
"Laughing Chorus" in *Der Freyschutz* [*sic*]
"Bertha"
"Henry"
"Caroline"
"Giovinetto Cavalier"
"The Plain Gold Ring"
"The Huntsman's Chorus" in *Der Freischutz* [*sic*]

Folder C

Collection of miscellaneous pieces of sheet music for voice and pianoforte, some being separate sheet issues and some excerpts from other collections. They are in very bad shape. Someone has stitched them together with string. The following list includes whatever is known about each selection.

"Time." A favorite sonnet composed by Pleyel. This particular edition was published in Dublin by Edmund Lee, No. 2 Dame st., near the Royal Exchange. Americans knew it as "Sonnet to Time" and it appeared in published American collections, [ca. 1799–1803].

"How Sweet the Love that Meets Return." Composed by Mr. Hook and sung by Mrs. Kennedy. Sonneck lists no known place or date of publication, but places it sometime in the 1790s.

"Ca Ira." French and English words. Published by Edmund Lee. Several American editions of this were available, 1793–96.

"Come Blushing Rose." By Pleyel, published by Edmund Lee. Published in America in 1795.

"From Branch to Branch." From the opera *Lionel and Clarissa*, music by Dibdin, libretto by Bickerstaff. This separate sheet published by Anne Lee, same address as Edmund Lee. The opera was performed in Philadelphia in 1792, and in various places through the 1790s.

"Poor Jack." By Charles Dibdin. No identification on this sheet, but several editions of the song were published in America, 1794–98.

"Ariette de Blaise et Babet." From *Blaise et Babet*, by N. Dezède. Words in French. No identification. Several American editions of the Overture from *Blaise et Babet* were published in America, 1789–1800.

"My Heavy Heart." A favorite Scotch song sung by Miss Bertles, VauxHall. Page no. 21 appears in upper right-hand corner. This indicates that it could be from *A Collection of Favorite Songs, Divided into Two Books*. Arranged by Alexander Reinagle. Published, Philadelphia, [ca. 1789].

"Canzonet" (1st line: "Time has not thinned my flowing hair . . ."). Composed by W. Jackson. No. 22 in upper left-hand corner identifies it as the back of the preceding page from Reinagle's book. Apparently, it had another page, which is missing.

"Donald." A favorite Scots song. No. 25 in upper right-hand corner. No other identification.

"Moggy's Complaint of Jockey." No. 26 in upper left-hand corner on the back of the previous page. No other identification.

Folder D

Pieces of music from a book of B. F. Peale's arrangement for Spanish Guitar, published by G. E. Blake of Philadelphia, July 29, 1826. Jefferson's granddaughters, Cornelia Randolph, Virginia Randolph Trist, and Septimia Randolph Meikleham, all played the guitar. Jefferson bought Virginia an expensive Spanish guitar in 1816, and there are many passages in the family correspondence that mention the fact that she played it, probably rather well. The date of this guitar music indicates that it was very likely used by Virginia, and perhaps later by Cornelia and Septimia.

"Loudon's Bonnie Woods and Braes"
"Waters of Elle"
"The Castilian Maid"
"Come Chace That Starting Tear Away"
"Tis Love in the Heart"
"I'll Watch for Thee"
"Home" ["Home, Sweet Home"]
"The Harper's Song"
"Slowly Wears the Day, Love"

Folder E

One-page manuscript fragment, "Row Gently Here—A Popular Venetian Air, from [?]." Piano and voice arrangement, with lyric.

Folder F

One-page sheet, "Flutt'ring Spread Thy Purple Pinions." Piano and voice, with guitar and German flute parts. Published by John Lee, No. 70 Dame St., at the corner of Eustace St., Dublin, [ca. 1778–1803].

Folder G

Two pieces of sheet music, bound together with string.

"The Timid Tear" Words by Moore, music by Barry. Piano and voice. Published by G. E. Blake, No. 1 South 3rd. St., Philadelphia, [1803/04–1814].

"In Praise of the Fair" Adapted to the popular French air, "La Pipe de Tobac." Piano and voice, with flute accompaniment. Also published by Blake. G. E. Blake came to the United States in 1793. These two pieces were probably published [ca. 1803–14].

Folder H

Miscellaneous pieces of manuscript music and lyrics in various hands, one of them Martha Jefferson Randolph's.

"Copenhagen Waltz with Variations"

"Cottage Rondo" composed by Holst

"The Tyrolese Song of Liberty" by Thomas Moore. Begins on last line of page where "Cottage Rondo" ends. The next page may be part of it; it has the same key and time signatures.

"Mozart's Favorite Waltz." Starts in the middle of the back of the previous page; it may or may not be by Moore.

"Robin Adair."

"Musette de Nina."

"The Coronach." Words by Scott, music by Dr. Clarke of Cambridge.

One page of manuscript lyrics;

"The Ill Wife" [verses 2–6].

"Home, Sweet Home" [2 verses, in hand of Martha Jefferson Randolph, inscribed "Tufton, April 2nd, 1827"].

"There's Nae Luck About the House" [verses 2–5].

Folder I

Fragment of a book of Scotch songs. Pp. v–vi of introduction, the table of contents, nos. 1–24 of the lyrics, and nos. 1–23 of the music are intact. Published, Blair-Sweet, Edinburgh, May 1, 1793.

Folder J

Six Ariettes Choisis, Avec Accompagnement D'un Clavecin ou Piano Forte Arrange Par Mr. L. Prix 4 livre 4 sols A Paris. Chez le Sr. Sieber Musicien rue St. Honore entre la rue D'orlean et Celle des vielles Etuves vis avis l'Hotel D'Aligre chez l'Apothicaire No. 92.

Air de *Chimene* ("Toi qui seul peut lire en mon coeur")

Air de *Didon* ("Ah! que je fus bien inspiree")

Air de *Chimene* ("Par donnes mon coeur vous offence")

Air de Rodrigue dans *Chimene* ("Tout ce qui dut me rendre heureux tout ce que j'maimais dans la vie")

De l'*Acte de Tibule et Delie* ("Je me prisais l'Amour")

Air de l'*Epreuve Villageoise* ("Bon Dieu com heir a cete fete")

Folder K

Miscellaneous sheets from several issues of a weekly music journal published in Paris. Voice and piano, or harpsichord.

Air from *Dardanus* ("Jour heureux") 2nd year, No. 17.

Airs de Ballet d'*Alexandre aux Indies* [same as above]

Air d'*Oedipe à Colone* [Sacchini] ("Votre cour devint mon azile") 3rd year, No. 19

Air de *Dardanus* ("C'est un charme supreme qui suspendra mon tourment") No. 44.

APPENDIX III

Thomas Jefferson's Violins?

OCCASIONALLY a violin purported to have belonged to Thomas Jefferson comes to light, then returns to join its fellows and an elusive Tourte violin bow in a limbo of nonprovenance. Their stories are often partly credible and always interesting.[1] Often the proud owner insists that his treasure is the Randolph violin, not having read the correspondence in the Library of Congress relating how the Randolph violin was sent to England for sale. Visitors to Monticello frequently ask about Jefferson's violins, wondering why there are none on display in the house after having read news items stating that various people believe themselves owners of violins from the former president's collection. There will probably not be a Jefferson violin on display at Monticello until somebody shows up with one with an impeccably documented story.

A violin known today as the Thomas-Malloy violin came to the attention of the Thomas Jefferson Memorial Foundation during the 1930s. Its owner offered it to the foundation for $12,000, claiming that Jefferson had given it to the owner's ancestor, Robert Warner Thomas, and that it was the Randolph violin. Robert Warner Thomas was the grandson of Jefferson's friend, Nicholas Lewis, and was raised by Mrs. Lewis. The family story is that Jefferson was a frequent visitor to the Lewis home during a time when little Robert was confined to bed with a long childhood illness. Jefferson, knowing of the boy's love for music, brought him one of his own violins and told him that he could keep it if he would learn to play it. The boy did learn to play quite well and continued to enjoy the violin for the rest of his life. After his death, the Jefferson violin became a treasured heirloom of his family.

Appraisers of the Thomas violin euphemistically called it an "interesting" old eighteenth-century German violin, certainly not of spectacular value. The most generous estimate by an examining expert was that it would have a rather nice tone and be worth about $200–$250 after $150 worth of repairs and restoration. A new fingerboard was one of the items that figured in the restoration. Around

[1] I wish to thank Mr. James A. Bear, Jr., Curator of Monticello, for making available to me material from the Monticello Archives for this appendix.

1860 the old fingerboard had worn out, and a repairer had replaced it with one made from the shinbone of a horse.

After the foundation decided not to buy the violin, its owner offered it for sale at Parke-Bernet in New York in 1940. Even when publicized as a Jefferson violin, it sold for only twenty dollars. The horrified former owner tried unsuccessfully to repossess it. The new owner, a Mr. John Malloy of Los Angeles, donated it to the foundation in 1957. The Thomas-Malloy instrument, complete with its unorthodox fingerboard, has the most believable story of any of the "Jefferson violins," however, the family's claim that it is the Randolph violin makes its provenance suspect. It is quite possible that Thomas Jefferson could have given an ordinary German violin to a young friend, especially if, as seems likely, he owned several such instruments, but it is ridiculous to think that he would have casually given away a valuable violin whose sale might financially benefit his family.

An instrument known as the Clark violin received much publicity early in the present century as a Jefferson violin and was the subject of an article in *Life* magazine as late as 1947. It, too, claimed to be the Randolph violin. A collector of stringed instruments, Albert Hildebrandt of Baltimore, discovered it in Charlottesville in 1899. Having heard of an old violin belonging to a 93-year-old Negro, Hildebrandt investigated, and the Negro told him that he had inherited the violin from his father, who had been one of the Monticello slaves. Hildebrandt bought the violin, proclaimed it to be an instrument made by Nicola Amati ca. 1660, and occasionally lent it to soloists. He seems to have issued a number of unfounded stories about the instrument—that it was the Randolph violin and that it was Jefferson's "pet" instrument, with which he wooed and won his wife. Had he checked more thoroughly, he would have known that Jefferson did not acquire the Randolph violin until 1775, several years after he married Martha.

In 1913 Hildebrandt sold the violin to a dealer, who in turn sold it for $50,000 to William A. Clark, Jr., an amateur violinist and benefactor of the Los Angeles Philharmonic. Clark died in 1934 and willed the violin to his violin teacher, Edwin H. Clark, who offered it to the Thomas Jefferson Memorial Foundation for $35,000. At that time the foundation could not afford to spend that much money for a violin, especially one with such an unlikely story. There was no real evidence relating the violin to Jefferson and no proof that Randolph's violin had actually been an Amati. Again, it was unlikely that Jefferson would have given a slave such a valuable instrument.

There are several amusing letters in the Monticello Archives between Edwin Clark and various members of the foundation. In all of his letters, Edwin Clark went to great lengths to show that the only proper place for the violin was Monticello and how badly he wanted to see it there—at his price. At one point in the negotiations, he magnanimously lowered his price to $20,000. His widow inherited the violin at his death in 1945, and at this juncture the story becomes hazy. There is reason to believe that it is now, or once was, in the possession of the Music School of the University of Southern California, but inquiries have failed to produce any more additions to its story.

Another "Jefferson violin" came from a rural midwestern state, where it may or may not still be. Its owner contacted the foundation in 1954 with the story of an old family violin that had a label inside it reading "*T. Jefferson 1766*." The owner's grandfather got the violin ca. 1860 from an old Indian violin craftsman who lived on the Mississinewa River. Marie Kimball, then curator of Monticello, asked the man to send the violin to her husband, Fiske Kimball, at the Philadelphia Museum of Art, for expert examination and appraisal, and he did so in February 1955.

The year 1955 was a turbulent year for the Thomas Jefferson Memorial Foundation. Both Kimballs died—Mrs. Kimball in March after a long illness, and Mr. Kimball suddenly in September. The new curator of Monticello, James A. Bear, Jr., had an unusually heavy volume of unfinished business to sort out and settle, including the midwestern violin. A thick file of letters at the foundation, referring to the violin, traces its subsequent history. Kimball's house in Philadelphia had been robbed while the instrument was still there, but it was untouched; Kimball, distraught at his wife's death, wanted to offer the violin's owner a large amount of money for it; the owner quite rightly wanted to know where it was, requested it back, and wondered what happened to Kimball; the insurance company inquired as to whether or not they should continue to insure it; and an eccentric relative of the owner wrote a pointed letter claiming that the violin was hers and therefore no one had a right to sell it.

Eventually, appraisals by experts blasted even the remotest hopes that the violin was a Jefferson violin. It was a German violin of no significant value and not even of Jefferson's time. Marie Kimball had been too ill to carefully examine the label, but several other Jefferson scholars said that the signature on the label could not possibly be Jefferson's. This fit in nicely with the fact that an expert claimed that the label was of mid-nineteenth-century manufacture despite the date *1766* having been written on it. Mr. Bear sent all of this information and the violin back to the family, to whom it was a sentimental heirloom if not a Jefferson violin. Once in a while he still gets a letter from the eccentric relative, who claims to have the violin hidden away and who wants him to furnish her all of the proof that it is a Jefferson violin.

An old violin was recently brought to Mr. Bear at Monticello and left for appraisal and evaluation by a gentleman from the Washington, D.C., area. He had been a student at the University of Virginia in 1916, and while he was living in Charlottesville a local friend gave his mother the instrument. It was supposed to have been found among some articles of furniture purchased from a descendant of one of Jefferson's slaves. Burned into the inside of the back is the inscription: *Made by Tom Craddock/ June 7. 1766/ for Thomas Jefferson.* A violin expert says that the violin is old enough to have been made ca. 1766, but that it is of German make and that all of the material used in it is of German origin. Tom Craddock has not yet been identified; however, there are two entries in the account books of small unspecified amounts paid to a Tom Cradock, but the entries are for the years 1811 and 1812. Time and, hopefully, more evidence will tell whether or not this might really be a Jefferson violin. It has a reasonable history.

The Tourte bow first appeared in public in February 1971 at an exhibition of French violin bows at the Lincoln Center's Library and Museum of the Performing Arts in New York. The bow was publicized in the exhibit as having belonged to Thomas Jefferson, but nobody furnished any documentation for Jefferson's ownership of it. It was on display again in October 1972 at Rembert Wurlitzer, Inc., in New York, probably the most famous violin dealer in the United States. Wurlitzer's very kindly furnished all the information they had for the bow, but unfortunately they had no more than Lincoln Center. It is possible that Jefferson could have owned one of these masterpieces of the bowmaker's art, but attempts to document his connection with this particular one have so far proved unsuccessful.

Glossary

CELESTINE APPARATUS (also called CELESTINE STOP or CELESTINA): one of several eighteenth-century devices which attempted to give a sustained, or bowed-string sound to keyboard instruments with plucked strings. The "bow" was a continuous moving band, against which the instrument's strings were pressed to make the sound. The celestina on Patsy Jefferson's harpsichord used rosined silk bands. Another form of "bow" was the round horsehair loop (ringbow) used in John Isaac Hawkins's claviol. See pp. 74–75.

CLAVICHORD: a rectangular keyboard instrument possessing metal blades (tangents) which strike the strings and produce the sound. Clavichords of Jefferson's day had no legs and were placed on stands or tables.

FLAGEOLET: a small vertical flute with a mouthpiece, somewhat like a recorder.

GLASS HARMONICA (or armonica): a series of glass basins of different pitches and graded sizes, fixed on a horizontal spindle made to revolve by a foot treadle. The spindle revolves in a trough containing enough water to keep the rims of the glasses wet. The performer produces the sound by stroking the wet, revolving rims of the glasses.

HARPSICHORD: a stringed keyboard instrument in which the sound is produced by jacks that pluck the strings. Harpsichords come in many sizes and are shaped somewhat like a grand piano. The strings are parallel to the straight side of the case.

JACK: the mechanical part of the harpsichord that plucks the strings. Depressing a key raises its corresponding jack and sets the mechanism in motion to pluck the string.

PLECTRUM: the material that projects from the jack and actually plucks the harpsichord's strings. In Jefferson's time, plectra were usually made of crow or raven quill; today they are made of leather or Delrin plastic.

SPINET: a very small triangular or polygonal harpsichord with strings running at an angle to the front. Spinets, like clavichords, were legless and sat on stands or tables.

VENETIAN SWELL: a series of narrow wooden louvers (very much like a Venetian blind) which were built over the top of a harpsichord's case. The performer operated a device which opened or closed the louvers, to give the harpsichord a louder or softer sound.

Bibliography

Manuscript Material Pertaining to TJ

Coolidge, Ellen Wayles Randolph [Mrs. Joseph Coolidge, Jr.]. The Ellen Wayles Coolidge Correspondence. Manuscripts Department, Alderman Library, University of Virginia.

The Edgehill Randolph Papers. Manuscripts Department, Alderman Library, University of Virginia.

———. Microfilmed by M.I.T. Microfilm in Library of Congress.

Jefferson, Thomas. Additional Files. Transcripts and photostats acquired from other depositories and private owners. Manuscripts Department, Alderman Library, University of Virginia.

———. Holograph book catalogue contained in one bound volume. March 6, 1783. Original, Massachusetts Historical Society. Photostats in Library of Congress and University of Virginia.

———. Catalogue. Undated holograph book catalogue, presumed to be a catalogue of acquisitions during Jefferson's residence in France. Original, Massachusetts Historical Society. Available on microfilm (reel #27 of the Coolidge Collection) at the University of Virginia.

———. Fee Book and Miscellaneous Accounts. Xerox, Curator's Office, Monticello. Original, Henry E. Huntington Library and Art Gallery, San Marino, California.

———. Ledger, 1767–1770. Xerox, Curator's Office, Monticello. Original, Henry E. Huntington Library and Art Gallery, San Marino, California.

———. Memorandum Book, 1773. Library of Congress. Photostats in Manuscripts Department, Alderman Library, University of Virginia.

———. Miscellaneous Accounts, 1764–79. Xerox, Curator's Office, Monticello. Originals, Henry E. Huntington Library and Art Gallery, San Marino, California.

———. Scrapbook. Miscellaneous collection of songs and poems pasted in scrapbooks by his granddaughters; Rare Book Room, Alderman Library, University of Virginia.

———. The Thomas Jefferson Papers. Manuscripts Department, Alderman Library, University of Virginia.

———. The Thomas Jefferson Papers. Coolidge Collection, Massachusetts Historical Society, Manuscripts Department, Alderman Library, University of Virginia.

———. The Thomas Jefferson Papers. Henry E. Huntington Library and Art Gallery, San Marino, California.

———. The Thomas Jefferson Papers. Library of Congress, Washington, D.C. Microfilm in Manuscripts Department, Alderman Library, University of Virginia.

The Meikleham-Randolph Papers. Manuscripts Department, Alderman Library, University of Virginia.

Meikleham, Septimia Ann Randolph [Mrs. David Meikleham]. The Septimia Randolph Meikleham Papers. Manuscripts Department, Alderman Library, University of Virginia.

Miscellaneous Cash Accounts. This account book covers the years 1767–1848 and contains many memoranda and accounts in several different hands. It contains a 23-page section of accounts, August 1767–June 1770, in Thomas Jefferson's hand. Manuscripts Department, Alderman Library, University of Virginia.

Papers of the Jefferson, Randolph, Taylor, Smith, and Nicholas Families. Acc. No. 8937, Manuscripts Department, Alderman Library, University of Virginia.

Thomas Jefferson's Account Books, 1767–1826. Typescript by James A. Bear, Jr. 5 vols., 2-vol. index. Manuscripts Department, Alderman Library, University of Virginia.

Trist, Nicholas Philip. The Nicholas Philip Trist Papers. Library of Congress.

———. The Nicholas Philip Trist Papers. The Southern Historical Collection, University of North Carolina Library.

Tucker-Coleman Papers, Earl Gregg Swem Library, College of William and Mary.

Washington, George. The George Washington Papers. University of Pennsylvania. Photostat at University of Virginia.

Wilson Cary Nicholas—Edgehill Randolph Papers. Acc. No. 5533, Manuscripts Department, Alderman Library, University of Virginia.

Collections of Music Belonging to the Jefferson Family

Jefferson Music. Eleven folders of music contemporary with Jefferson and connected with him. Photostats and xerox copies from various depositories. Rare Book Room, Alderman Library, University of Virginia.

Manuscript Music Book of Songs and Miscellaneous Pieces. Supposedly belonged to Martha Jefferson Randolph. Approximately 111 pp. in book, 3 pp. unidentifiable printed music, MS. pp. 2–111. Acc. No. 7443–f, Manuscripts Department, Alderman Library, University of Virginia.

Monticello Music Collection. Six boxes and one oversize box of music that belonged to Thomas Jefferson, his wife, daughters, and granddaughters. Instrumental, vocal, and miscellaneous manuscript fragments. Acc. No. 3177, Manuscripts Department, Alderman Library, University of Virginia.

———. Small collection of miscellaneous pieces of French, English, and American editions of sheet music and fragments of music books; a few manuscript copies, some in the handwriting of Martha Jefferson Randolph. Office of the curator of Monticello. Curator's Accession No. 71–6331.

Music from the Library of Thomas Jefferson. A collection of 18th-century songs, chiefly vocal music. Autograph: John Wayles, father-in-law of Thomas Jefferson. Rare Book Room, Alderman Library, University of Virginia.

Music Manuscript Notebook [ca. 1770]. This notebook allegedly belonged to Martha Wayles Skelton Jefferson. Into it have been copied words and music of several songs. Deposited with the Manuscripts Department of the University of Virginia Library by Mr. James A. Bear., curator of Monticello.

Randolph, Jane Cary Harrison. *Thomas Jefferson: Monticello Music, 1785*. St. Louis: Cary H. Randolph, [1941].

Published Collections of TJ's Writings

Betts, Edwin Morris, ed. *Thomas Jefferson's Garden Book*. Philadelphia: American Philosophical Society, 1944.

———, and James A. Bear, Jr., eds. *The Family Letters of Thomas Jefferson*. Columbia, Mo.: University of Missouri Press, 1966.

Boyd, Julian P. et al., eds. *The Papers of Thomas Jefferson*. 17 vols. Princeton, N.J.: Princeton University Press, 1950–.

Cappon, Lester J., ed. *The Adams-Jefferson Letters*. 2 vols. Chapel Hill, N.C.: University of North Carolina Press, 1959.

Jefferson, Thomas. *Notes on the State of Virginia*. New York: Harper and Row, 1964.

Lipscomb, Andrew A., and Albert Ellery Bergh, eds. *The Writings of Thomas Jefferson*. Washington, D.C.: Thomas Jefferson Memorial Association, 1903–1904.

Primary Sources

Adams, Charles Francis, ed. *Memoirs of John Quincy Adams.* 12 vols. Philadelphia: J. B. Lippincott, 1874–77.

Bacon, Capt. Edmund. "Jefferson at Monticello: The Private Life of Thomas Jefferson." In *Jefferson At Monticello.* Ed. James A. Bear, Jr. Charlottesville, Va.: University Press of Virginia, 1967.

Brown, Marvin L., Jr., trans. and ed. *Baroness von Riedesel and the American Revolution.* Chapel Hill, N.C.: University of North Carolina Press, 1965.

Carson, Jane. *We Were There.* Williamsburg, Va.: Colonial Williamsburg, Inc., 1965.

Catalogue of the Library of Congress, December 1830. Washington, D.C.: Duff Green, 1830.

Chastellux, Jean-François, Marquis de. *Travels in North America in the Years 1780, 1781, 1782.* Trans. and ed. Howard C. Rice, Jr. 2 vols. Chapel Hill, N.C.: University of North Carolina Press, 1963.

"Diary of Mrs. William Thornton, 1800–1863." *Records of the Columbia Historical Society* 10 (1907): 88–226.

Dix, Morgan, comp. *Memoirs of John Adams Dix.* 2 vols. New York: Harper and Brothers, 1883.

Eelking, Max von. *Memoirs, and Letters and Journals, of Major General Riedesel, During His Residence in America.* Trans. William L. Stone. 2 vols. Albany: J. Munsell, 1868.

1828 Catalogue of the Library of the University of Virginia. Reproduced in facsimile. Introduction by William H. Peden. Charlottesville, Va.: University of Virginia Press, 1945.

Foster, Sir Augustus John. *Jeffersonian America. Notes on the United States of America, Collected in the years 1805–6–7 and 1811–12.* Ed. Richard Beale Davis. San Marino, Calif.: Huntington Library, 1954.

Gibbs, George, ed. *Memoirs of the Administrations of Washington and John Adams.* Edited from the papers of Oliver Wolcott, Secretary of the Treasury. 1846. Reprint. New York: Burt Franklin, 1971.

Gray, Francis Calley [1790–1856]. *Thomas Jefferson in 1814.* Ed. Henry S. Rowe and Thomas Jefferson Coolidge, Jr. Boston: The Club of Odd Volumes, 1924.

Hodgson, Adam. *Letters from North America. . . .* London: Hurst, Robinson, 1824.

Hunt, Galliard, ed. *The First Forty Years of Washington Society: In the Family Letters of Margaret Bayard Smith.* 1906. Reprint. New York: Frederick Ungar, 1965.

Hunter, Robert, Jr. *Quebec to Carolina in 1785–86.* Ed. L. B. Wright and Marion Tingling. San Marino, Calif.: Huntington Library, 1943.

Janson, Charles William. *The Stranger in America, 1792–1806*. Ed. Carl S. Driver. 1807. Reprint. New York: The Press of the Pioneers, 1935.

Jefferson, Isaac. "Memoirs of a Monticello Slave." In *Jefferson At Monticello*. Ed. James A. Bear, Jr. Charlottesville, Va.: University Press of Virginia, 1967.

Johansson, Cari. *French Music Publishers' Catalogues of the Second Half of the Eighteenth Century*. Malmö, Sweden: A. B. Malmö Ljustrycksanstalt, 1945.

Labaree, Leonard W. et al., eds. *The Papers of Benjamin Franklin, Vol. 10, January 1, 1762 through December 31, 1763*. New Haven: Yale University Press, 1966.

Marraro, H. R., ed. *Memoirs of the Life of Philip Mazzei*. New York: Columbia University Press, 1942.

Mason, Francis, ed. *John Norton and Sons, Merchants of London and Virginia, 1750–1795*. Richmond: Dietz, 1937.

Mayo, Bernard, ed. *Thomas Jefferson and His Unknown Brother Randolph*. Charlottesville, Va.: University of Virginia Press, 1942.

Praetorius, Michael. *Syntagma Musicum, 1615–20*. Vol. II, *De Organographia*, 1st and 2nd parts. Trans. Harold Blumenfeld. New Haven: Chinese Printing Office, Yale University, 1949.

Prime, A. C. *Arts and Crafts in Philadelphia, Maryland, and South Carolina 1721–1785*. 2 vols. The Walpole Society, 1929.

Randall, Henry S. *The Life of Thomas Jefferson*. 3 vols. New York: Derby and Jackson, 1858.

Randolph, Sarah N. *The Domestic Life of Thomas Jefferson*. Charlottesville, Va.: Thomas Jefferson Memorial Foundation, 1967.

Royall, Mrs. Anne. *Mrs. Royall's Southern Tour, or Second Series of the Black Book*. 3 vols. Washington, D.C.: [no publisher] 1830.

Scholes, Percy A., ed. *Dr. Burney's Musical Tours in Europe*. Vol. I, *An Eighteenth-Century Musical Tour in France and Italy*. London: Oxford University Press, 1959.

Newspapers

Dunlap's American Daily Advertiser (Philadelphia), selected issues.

Journal de Paris, Sept. 1784–Sept. 1789.

The London Chronicle, Mar.–Apr. 1786.

The Maryland Journal and Baltimore Advertiser, Vol. X, No. 4 [no. 491], Tuesday, Jan. 28, 1783.

The National Intelligencer (Washington, D.C.), selected issues.

Philadelphia Aurora and General Advertiser, selected issues.

The Virginia Gazette. Published in Williamsburg, Virginia, by: Alexander Purdie and John Dixon, 1766–75; William Rind, 1766–73; Clementina Rind, 1773–74; John Dixon and William Hunter, Jr., 1775–78; John Pinkney, 1774–76; Alexander Purdie, 1775–79; John Dixon and Thomas Nicolson, 1779–Apr. 1780; John Clarkson and Augustine Davis, 1779–Dec. 1780.

Indexes, Catalogues, Bibliographies, Calendars

Apel, Willi and Ralph T. Daniel, eds. *The Harvard Brief Dictionary of Music*. Cambridge, Mass.: Harvard University Press, 1960.

Baker's Biographical Dictionary of Musicians. 5th rev. ed. Ed. Nicholas Slominsky. New York: G. Schirmer, 1958.

Bio-Bibliographical Index of Musicians in the United States of America Since Colonial Times. District of Columbia Historical Records Survey. Music Section, Pan American Union. Washington, D.C.: Music Division, Library of Congress, 1956.

The British Union-Catalogue of Early Music Printed Before the Year 1801. Ed. Edith B. Schnapper. 2 vols. London: Butterworth's Scientific Publications, 1957.

Dichter, Harry and Elliott Shapiro. *Early American Sheet Music: Its Lure and Its Lore, 1768–1889*. New York: R. R. Bowker, 1941.

Fétis, F. J. *Biographie Universelle des Musiciens et Bibliographie Générale de la Musique*. Deuxième Edition. Paris: Librarie de Firmin Didot, Frères, Fils et Cie., 1869–73. Supplement et complement, 1878–80.

Grove's Dictionary of Music and Musicians. 5th rev. ed. Ed. Eric Blom. New York: St. Martin's Press, 1970. *American Supplement*. Ed. Waldo Selden Pratt. Philadelphia: Theodore Presser, 1922.

Hogan, Charles B., ed. *The London Stage, 1660–1800: Part 5, 1776–1800*. Carbondale, Ill.: Southern Illinois University Press, 1968.

Hopkinson, Cecil. *A Dictionary of Parisian Music Publishers, 1700–1950*. London: Cecil Hopkinson, 1954.

Hughes, Rupert, comp. *Music Lovers' Encyclopedia*. 1903. Rev. and ed. Deems Taylor and Russell Kerr. Garden City: Garden City Books, 1950.

Humphries, Charles and William C. Smith. *Music Publishing in the British Isles*. New York: Barnes and Noble, 1970.

The Jefferson Cyclopedia. Ed. John P. Foley. New York: Funk and Wagnells, 1900.

Johansson, Cari. *French Music Publishers' Catalogues of the Second Half of the Eighteenth Century*. Stockholm: Library of the Royal Swedish Academy of Music, 1955.

Library of the University of Virginia. Jefferson Calendar Supplement. 2 vols. 1769–1808, 1808–n.d. Manuscripts Department, University of Virginia Library (typescript).

Redway, Virginia Larkin. *Music Directory of Early New York City.* New York: New York Public Library, 1941.

Rees, Abraham. *Dr. Rees's New Cyclopaedia* . . . Vol. IX, Part 1. Philadelphia: Robert Carr, 1810.

Russell, Raymond. *Catalogue of Musical Instruments. Volume I, Keyboard Instruments* [Victoria and Albert Museum]. London: Her Majesty's Stationery Office, 1968.

Sonneck, Oscar G. *A Bibliography of Early American Secular Music.* Rev. and enl. William Treat Upton. Washington, D.C.: Music Division, The Library of Congress, 1945.

Sowerby, E. Millicent, comp. *Catalogue of the Library of Thomas Jefferson.* 5 vols. Washington, D.C.: U.S. Government Printing Office, 1955.

Thurlow, Constance and Francis Berkeley, eds. *The Jefferson Papers of the University of Virginia.* Charlottesville, Va.: University of Virginia Press, 1950.

Tyler, Lyon G., ed. *Encyclopedia of Virginia Biography.* 4 vols. New York: Lewis Historical Publishing Company, 1915.

University of Virginia. *Fourteenth Annual Report on Historical Collections at the University of Virginia Library, 1943–1944.* Charlottesville, Va.: University of Virginia Press, 1944, pp. 27–28.

———. *Tenth Annual Report on Historical Collections at the University of Virginia Library 1939–40.* Charlottesville, Va.: University of Virginia Press, 1940, p. 8.

———. *Twentieth Annual Report on Historical Collections at the University of Virginia Library 1949–50.* Charlottesville, Va.: University of Virginia Press, 1951, pp. 286–94.

Webster's Biographical Dictionary. Springfield, Mass.: G. and C. Merriam, 1943.

Wolfe, Richard J., ed. *Secular Music in America, 1801–1825. A Bibliography.* 3 vols. New York: New York Public Library, 1964.

Miscellaneous Pamphlets, Clippings, Bulletins

Bear, James A., Jr. *Jefferson's Advice to His Children and Grandchildren on Their Reading.* Charlottesville, Va.: Tracy W. McGregor Library, 1967.

"A Checklist of Keyboard Instruments at the Smithsonian Institution." Division of Musical Instruments, Museum of History and Technology, Washington, D.C.

"Founder's Day Concert" by the Glee Club assisted by members of the Concert Band in honor of the two-hundredth anniversary of the birth of Thomas Jefferson. April 13, 1943. University of Virginia, Division of Music. Program notes by Helen Duprey Bullock.

Kimball, Marie. *The Furnishings of Monticello.* [Philadelphia (?), 1941].

"Museum gets Jefferson's music books." Photostat copy from *Music Trade News*, August 1931, p. 18, held by the Rare Books Room, Alderman Library, University of Virginia.

Rice, H. C. *L'Hotel de Langeac, Jefferson's Paris Residence, 1785–1789.* Paris and Monticello: Thomas Jefferson Memorial Foundation, 1947.

Schonberg, Harold C. "Favorite Passion." *New York Times*, November 19, 1961.

Unpublished Materials

Armstrong, Susan. "A Repertoire of the American Colonial Theater." MS. report in Research Department, The Colonial Williamsburg Foundation.

Bear, James A., Jr. Chronology. Typescript giving itineraries and lengths of residence in various places of Thomas Jefferson, his wife Martha, and his daughters, Martha Jefferson Randolph and Maria Jefferson Eppes. Curator's Office, Monticello.

———. Thomas Jefferson Itinerary Index. Xerox copy, Manuscripts Department, Alderman Library, University of Virginia.

Benson, Norman Arthur. "The Itinerant Dancing and Music Masters of Eighteenth Century America." Ph.D. dissertation. University of Minnesota, 1963.

Betts, Edwin Morris. "Jefferson: Gardening and Music." Typescript, Manuscripts Department, Alderman Library, University of Virginia.

Brent, Robert Arthur. "Nicholas Philip Trist's Search for a Career." M.A. thesis. University of Virginia, 1947.

Bullock, Helen Duprey. "On Music in Colonial Williamsburg." MS. report in Research Department, The Colonial Williamsburg Foundation.

Covey, Cyclone. "Religion and Music in Colonial America." Ph.D. dissertation. Stanford University, 1949.

Goodwin, Mary. "Musical Instruments in Eighteenth Century America." MS. report in Research Department, The Colonial Williamsburg Foundation.

———. "Thomas Jefferson's Association with Williamsburg." MS. report in Research Department, The Colonial Williamsburg Foundation.

Haskins, John C. "Music in the District of Columbia, 1800 to 1814." M.A. thesis. Catholic University, 1952.

McClellan, Major Edwin North. "The U.S. Marine Band." 21-page typescript, Music Division, Library of Congress.

Maurer, Maurer. "The Musical Life of Colonial America in the Eighteenth Century." Ph.D. dissertation. Ohio State University, 1950.

Nolan, Carolyn Galbraith. "Thomas Jefferson: Gentleman Musician." M.A. thesis. University of Virginia, 1967.

Peden, William. "Thomas Jefferson: Book Collector." Ph.D. dissertation. University of Virginia, 1942.

Pulley, Judith ."Thomas Jefferson at the Court of Versailles: An American *Philosophe* and the Coming of the French Revolution." Ph.D. dissertation. University of Virginia, 1966.

Stoutamire, Albert L. "A History of Music in Richmond, Virginia, from 1742 to 1865." Ph.D. dissertation. Florida State University, 1960.

Articles

Allan, Alfred K. "The Music Lover of Monticello." *Music Journal* 13 (1955): 39, 58.

"An Eighteenth-Century Directory of London Musicians." *Galpin Society Journal* 2 (1949):27–31.

Antrim, Doron K. "Our Musical Presidents." *Etude*, May 1940, pp. 229+.

Babitz, Sol. "Recent Findings in 18th-Century Performance Style." *American String Teacher* (winter, 1965): 10–15.

Benton, Rita. "The Early Piano in the United States." In *Music Libraries and Instruments*. London: Hinrichsen's Eleventh Music Book, 1961. Pp. 179–89.

Biancolli, Louis. "Thomas Jefferson, Fiddler." *Life* 22 (1947): 13–20.

Boston, Canon Noel. "The Barrel Organ." *Music Libraries and Instruments*. London: Hinrichsen's Eleventh Music Book, 1961. Pp. 200–204.

Boyden, David D. "The Violin and Its Technique in the 18th Century." *Musical Quarterly* 36 (1950): 9–38.

Bullock, Helen Duprey. "A Dissertation on Education in the Form of a Letter from James Maury to Robert Jackson, July 17, 1762." *Papers of the Albemarle County Historical Society*, 2 (1941–42): 36–60.

———. "Mr. Jefferson—Musician." *Etude*, October 1943, pp. 633+.

———. "The Papers of Thomas Jefferson." *American Archivist* 4 (1941): 238–49.

Butterfield, L. H. and Howard C. Rice, Jr. "Jefferson's Earliest Note to Maria Cosway with Some New Facts and Conjectures on His Broken Wrist." *William and Mary Quarterly* 5 (1948): 26–33.

Covey, Cyclone. "Of Music and of America Singing." In *Seeds of Liberty.* Ed. Max Savelle. New York: Alfred A. Knopf, 1948.

Daniel, Frederick. "Virginian Reminiscences of Jefferson." *Harper's Weekly* 48 (1904): 1766–68.

Daniel, Ralph T. "Handel Publications in 18th-Century America." *Musical Quarterly* 45 (1959): 168–74.

"Diary of John Blair" [1751]. *William and Mary Quarterly* 7 (1898–99): 133–53.

Dinneen, William. "Early American Manuscript Music-Books." *Musical Quarterly* 30 (1944): 50–62.

Ford, Paul L. "Thomas Jefferson in Undress." *Scribner's Magazine* 12 (1892): 509–16.

Garbett, Arthur S. "Thomas Jefferson's Lifelong Love of Music." *Etude*, August 1941, pp. 510+.

Gauss, Charles E. "Thomas Jefferson's Musical Interests." *Etude*, 51 (1933): 367+.

Gough, Hugh. "The Classical Grand Pianoforte, 1770–1830." *Proceedings of the Royal Musical Association* 77 (1950–51): 41–50.

Halfpenny, Eric. "An Eighteenth-Century Trade List of Musical Instruments." *Galpin Society Journal* 17 (1964): 99–102.

Harbrecht, Rosemary. "Thomas Jefferson: Man of Culture." *The Social Studies* 41 (1950): 258–60.

Henkels, Stan. V. "Jefferson's Recollections of Patrick Henry." *Pennsylvania Magazine of History and Biography* 34 (1910): 385–418.

Jeans, Susi. "The Pedal Clavichord and Other Practice Instruments of Organists." *Proceedings of the Royal Musical Association* 77 (1950–51): 1–15.

Johnson, H. Earle. "The Adams Family and Good Listening." *Journal of the American Musicological Society* 11 (1958): 165–76.

Kallen, H. M. "The Arts and Thomas Jefferson." *Ethics* 53: 269–83.

Kimball, Fiske. "Jefferson and the Arts." *Proceedings of the American Philosophical Society* 87 (1944): 238–45.

Kimball, Marie. "Jefferson in Paris." *North American Review* 248 (1940): 73–86.

———. "Jefferson's Farewell to Romance." *Virginia Quarterly Review* 4 (1928): 402–19.

———. "A Playmate of Thomas Jefferson." *North American Review* 213 (1921): 145–56.

———. "William Short, Jefferson's Only 'Son.'" *North American Review* 223 (1926): 471–86.

King, A. Hyatt. "The Musical Glasses and Glass Harmonica." *Proceedings of the Royal Musical Association* 72 (1946–47): 99–122.

Kuper, Theodore F. "Thomas Jefferson, Lover of Music." *Tempo* 1 (1934): 18.

La Laurencie, Lionel de. "Benjamin Franklin and the Claveciniste Brillon de Jouy." *Musical Quarterly* 9 (1923): 245–59.

"Letter of Anne Blair to Martha Braxton." *William and Mary Quarterly* 16 (1907–8): 174–80.

"Library of Col. Ralph Wormely, Esq." *William and Mary Quarterly* 2 (1893–94): 169–174.

"Library of Col. William Fleming." *William and Mary Quarterly* 6 (1897–98): 158–64.

"Library of Edmund Berkeley, Esq." *William and Mary Quarterly* 2 (1893–94): 250–51.

McAdie, Alexander. "Thomas Jefferson at Home." *Proceedings of the American Antiquarian Society* 40: 27–46.

McClellan, Major Edwin North. "How the Marine Band Started." Reprinted from the *U. S. Institute Proceedings* 49 (1923): 581–86.

Malone, Dumas. "Jefferson Goes to School in Williamsburg." *Virginia Quarterly Review* 33 (1957): 481–96.

———. "Polly Jefferson and Her Father." *Virginia Quarterly Review* 7 (1931): 81–95.

Maurer, Maurer. "The Library of a Colonial Musician, 1755." *William and Mary Quarterly* 7 (1950): 39–52.

———. "A Musical Family in Colonial Virginia." *Musical Quarterly* 34 (1948): 358–.

———. "Peter Pelham: Organist-Jailer." *Tyler's Quarterly Historical and Genealogical Magazine* 28 (1946): 6–13.

———. "The 'Professor of Musick' in Colonial America." *Musical Quarterly* 36 (1950): 511–24.

Mayo, Barbara. "Twilight at Monticello." *Virginia Quarterly Review* 17 (1941): 502–16.

Molnar, John W. "Art Music in Colonial Virginia." In *Art and Music in the South*. Ed. Francis B. Simkins. Longwood College Institute of Southern Cultural Lectures. Farmville, Va.: 1961.

———. "A Collection of Music in Colonial Virginia: The Ogle Library." *Musical Quarterly*, April 1963, 150–62.

Nathan, Hans. "Early Banjo Tunes and American Syncopation." *Musical Quarterly* 42 (1956): 455–72.

———. "United States of America." In *A History of Song*. Ed. Denis Stevens. New York: W. W. Norton, 1960.

Nicolay, John G. "Thomas Jefferson's Home." *Century Magazine* 34 (1887): 643–53.

Parrish, Carl. "Criticisms of the Piano When It Was New." *Musical Quarterly* 30 (1944): 428–40.

Parton, James. "College Days of Thomas Jefferson." *Atlantic Monthly* 29 (1872): 16–33.

Peden, William. "Some Notes Concerning Thomas Jefferson's Libraries." *William and Mary Quarterly* 1 (1944): 265–72.

Pierce, E. H. "Thomas Jefferson and His Violin." *Etude*, September 1929, 684–85.

Proctor, John Clagett. "Marine Band History and Its Leaders." Magazine Section, *Washington Sunday Star*, May 8, 1932, pp. 6+.

Randolph, Sarah N. "Mrs. Thomas Mann Randolph." In *Worthy Women of Our First Century*. Ed. Mrs. O. J. Wister and Agnes Irwin. Philadelphia: J. B. Lippincott, 1877.

Ratner, Leonard G. "Eighteenth-Century Theories of Musical Period Structure." *Musical Quarterly* 42 (1956): 439–54.

Redway, Virginia Larkin. "The Carrs, American Music Publishers." *Musical Quarterly* 18 (1932): 150–77.

"Sarah Hallam." *William and Mary Quarterly* 12 (1903–4): 236–37.

Schonberg, H. C. "Jefferson and the Piano." *Piano Teacher* 4 (1962): 11–12.

Sewall, Maude G. "Washington and Its Musical History." *Music Teachers National Association, Proceedings* 27 (1932): 35–44.

Shepperson, Archibald B. "Thomas Jefferson Visits England and Buys a Harpsichord." In *Humanistic Studies in Honor of James Calvin Metcalf*. University of Virginia Studies. Charlottesville, Va.: University of Virginia Press, 1941.

Sterling, Peter R. "Society in Jefferson's Day." *National Republic* 17 (1929): 28.

Stockton, Frank R. "The Later Years of Monticello." *Century Magazine* 34 (1887): 654–57.

Taylor, Olivia. "Dear Ghosts of Lego and Monticello." *Papers of the Albemarle County Historical Society* 3 (1942–43): 17–32.

Tyler, Lyon G., ed. "Libraries in Colonial Virginia." Part II. *William and Mary Quarterly* 3 (1894–95): 251–53.

Wayland, John W. "The Poetical Tastes of Thomas Jefferson." *Sewanee Review* 18 (1910): 283–99.

Whistler, Harvey S. and Georgeanna K. Whistler. "François Tourte: Bow Maker Supreme." Part 1, *Music Journal*, May 1965, 27, 75–77; Part 2, *ibid.*, September 1965, 45–46, 78–79.

Wilstach, Paul. "Thomas Jefferson's Little Mountain." *National Geographic* 55 (1929): 481–503.

"The World of Music." *Etude*, September 1929, 639.

Zimmerman, Ruth. "The String's the Thing." *American String Teacher* (fall, 1964): 14–15.

Books

Apel, Willi. *Masters of the Keyboard.* Cambridge, Mass.: Harvard University Press, 1947.

Ayars, Christine Merrick. *Contributions to the Art of Music in America by the Music Industries of Boston, 1640 to 1936.* New York: H. W. Wilson, 1937.

Baines, Anthony. *European and American Musical Instruments.* New York: The Viking Press, 1966.

———, ed. *Musical Instruments Through the Ages.* London: Penguin Books, 1961.

Benade, Arthur. *Horns, Strings, and Harmony.* Garden City: Doubleday, 1960.

Berman, Eleanor D. *Thomas Jefferson Among the Arts.* New York: Philosophical Library, 1947.

Boalch, Donald. *Makers of the Harpsichord and Clavichord 1440 to 1840.* New York: Macmillan, 1956.

Boorstin, Daniel J. *The Lost World of Thomas Jefferson.* Boston: Beacon Press, 1960.

Boyden, David B. *The History of Violin Playing from its Origins to 1761 and its Relationship to the Violin and Violin Music.* London: Oxford University Press, 1965.

Bridenbaugh, Carl and Jessica Bridenbaugh. *Rebels and Gentlemen: Philadelphia in the Age of Franklin.* New York: Oxford University Press, 1965.

Briqueville, Eugène de. *Un Coin de la Curiosité. Les Anciens Instruments de Musique.* Paris: Librarie de l'Art, 1894.

Brockway, Wallace and Herbert Weinstock. *Men of Music: Their Lives, Times, and Achievements.* New York: Simon and Schuster, 1939.

Bruce, Philip Alexander. *History of the University of Virginia 1819–1919.* 5 vols. New York: Macmillan, 1922.

Bryan, Wilhelmus B. *A History of the National Capital.* Vol. I, 1790–1814. New York: Macmillan, 1914.

Bukofzer, Manfred F. *Music in the Baroque Era: From Monteverdi to Bach.* New York: W. W. Norton, 1947.

Bullock, Helen Duprey. *My Head and My Heart.* New York: G. P. Putnam's, 1945.

Cabell, Nathaniel F., ed. *Early History of the University of Virginia.* Richmond, Va.: J. W. Randolph, 1856.

Carse, Adam. *The Orchestra in the Eighteenth Century.* Cambridge: W. Heffer; New York: Broude Brothers, 1940.

Carson, Jane. *Colonial Virginians at Play.* Williamsburg Research Studies. Williamsburg, Va.: Colonial Williamsburg, Inc., 1965.

Chase, Gilbert. *America's Music: From the Pilgrims to the Present.* New York: McGraw-Hill, 1955.

Cometti, Elizabeth, ed. *Jefferson's Ideas on a University Library.* Charlottesville, Va.: University of Virginia Press, 1950.

Culbreth, David M. *The University of Virginia; Memories of Her Student Life and Professors.* New York: The Neale Publishing Company, 1908.

Curtis, William E. *The True Thomas Jefferson.* Philadelphia: Lippincott, 1901.

Davidson, Peter. *The Violin: Its Construction Theoretically and Practically Treated.* London: F. Pitman, 1881.

Davis, Burke. *A Williamsburg Galaxy.* New York: Holt, Rinehart and Winston, for Colonial Williamsburg, 1968.

Davis, Richard Beale. *Intellectual Life in Jefferson's Virginia, 1790–1830.* Chapel Hill, N.C.: University of North Carolina Press, 1964.

Doring, Ernest N. *How Many Strads?* Chicago: William Lewis, 1945.

Ducros, Louis. *French Society in the Eighteenth Century.* London: G. Bell, 1926.

Dumbauld, Edward. *Thomas Jefferson, American Tourist.* Norman, Okla.: University of Oklahoma Press, 1946.

Editors of American Heritage. *Thomas Jefferson and His World.* Narrative by Henry Moscow, with Dumas Malone. New York: American Heritage, 1960.

Ewen, David. *The Story of America's Musical Theater.* Philadelphia: Chilton, 1961.

Fisher, William Arms. *One Hundred and Fifty Years of Music Publishing in the United States, 1783–1933.* Boston: Oliver Ditson, 1933.

Gagey, Edmond McAdoo. *Ballad Opera.* New York: Columbia University Press, 1937.

Gaines, William H., Jr. *Thomas Mann Randolph, Jefferson's Son-in-Law.* Baton Rouge, La.: Louisiana State University Press, 1966.

Galpin, Francis. *Old English Instruments of Music.* London: Methuen, 1910.

———. *A Textbook of European Musical Instruments.* London: Williams and Norgate, 1937.

Garrett, Wendell D. *Thomas Jefferson Redivivus.* Barre, Mass.: Barre Publishers, 1971.

Geiringer, Karl. *Musical Instruments*. Trans. Bernard Miall; ed. W. F. B. Blandford. New York: Oxford University Press, 1943.

Gerson, Robert A. *Music in Philadelphia*. Philadelphia: Theodore Presser, 1940.

Green, Constance M. *Washington, Village and Capitol, 1800–1878*. Vol. I. Princeton, N.J.: Princeton University Press, 1962.

Hall, Gordon Langley. *Mr. Jefferson's Ladies*. Boston: Beacon Press, 1966.

Hall, James Husst. *The Art Song*. Norman, Okla.: University of Oklahoma Press, 1953.

Hamel, Frank. *Famous French Salons*. New York: Brentano's, 1908.

Harding, Rosamund E. M. *The Pianoforte: Its History Traced to the Great Exhibition of 1851*. Cambridge: Cambridge University Press, 1933.

Harman, Alec and Anthony Milner. *Late Renaissance and Baroque Music (c. 1525–c. 1750)*. London: Barrie and Rockliff, 1959.

Hastings, George Everett. *The Life and Works of Francis Hopkinson*. Chicago: University of Chicago Press, 1926.

Heron-Allen, Edward. *Violin-Making As It Was and Is*. London: Ward, Lock, [1885].

Hill, W. Henry and Alfred E. Hill. *Antonio Stradivari: His Life and Work (1644–1737)*. 1902. Reprint. New York: Dover Publications, 1963.

Hipkins, A. J. *Musical Instruments: Historic, Rare and Unique*. Edinburgh: Adam and Charles Black, 1888.

Hirt, Franz Joseph. *Stringed Keyboard Instruments, 1440–1880*. Boston: Boston Book and Art Shop, 1968.

Hitchcock, H. Wiley. *Music in the United States: A Historical Introduction*. Englewood Cliffs, N.J.: Prentice-Hall, 1969.

Honeywell, Roy J. *The Educational Work of Thomas Jefferson*. Cambridge, Mass.: Harvard University Press, 1931.

Howard, John Tasker. *The Music of George Washington's Time*. Washington, D.C.: The United States George Washington Bicentennial Commission, 1931.

Hubbard, Frank. *Three Centuries of Harpsichord Making*. Cambridge, Mass.: Harvard University Press, 1965.

Hutchings, Arthur J. B. *The Baroque Concerto*. New York: W. W. Norton, 1965.

James, Philip. *Early Keyboard Instruments: From Their Beginnings to the Year 1820*. London: Peter Davies, 1930.

Keller, Hermann. *Thoroughbass Method*. Trans. and ed. Carl Parrish. New York: W. W. Norton, 1965.

Kenyon, Max. *Harpsichord Music*. London: Cassell, 1949.

Kimball, Marie. *Jefferson: The Road to Glory, 1743 to 1776.* New York: Coward-McCann, 1943.

———. *Jefferson: The Scene of Europe, 1784 to 1789.* New York: Coward-McCann, 1950.

———. *Jefferson: War and Peace, 1776 to 1784.* New York: Coward-McCann, 1947.

Koch, Adrienne and William Peden, eds. *The Life and Selected Writings of Thomas Jefferson.* New York: The Modern Library, 1944.

Lehmann, Karl. *Thomas Jefferson, American Humanist.* New York: Macmillan, 1947.

Loesser, Arthur. *Men, Women, and Pianos.* New York: Simon and Schuster, 1954.

Long, O. W. *Thomas Jefferson and George Ticknor: A Chapter in American Scholarship.* Williamstown, Mass., 1933.

Madeira, Louis C., comp. *Annals of Music in Philadelphia. . . .* Philadelphia: J. B. Lippincott, 1896.

Main, Jackson Turner. *The Social Structure of Revolutionary America.* Princeton, N.J.: Princeton University Press, 1965.

Malone, Dumas. *Jefferson and the Ordeal of Liberty.* Vol. III of *Jefferson and His Time.* Boston: Little, Brown, 1962.

———. *Jefferson and the Rights of Man.* Vol. II of *Jefferson and His Time.* Boston: Little, Brown, 1951.

———. *Jefferson the President: First Term, 1801–1805.* Vol. IV of *Jefferson and His Time.* Boston: Little, Brown, 1970.

———. *Jefferson the Virginian.* Vol. I of *Jefferson and His Time.* Boston: Little, Brown, 1948.

Marambaud, Pierre. *William Byrd of Westover.* Charlottesville, Va.: University Press of Virginia, 1971.

Mates, Julian. *The American Musical Stage Before 1800.* New Brunswick, N.J.: Rutgers University Press, 1962.

Miller, John C. *The Federalist Era, 1789–1801.* The New American National Series. Ed. Henry Steele Commager and Richard B. Morris. New York: Harper and Row, 1963.

Morgan, Edmund S. *Virginians at Home.* Charlottesville, Va.: University Press of Virginia, 1963.

Morton, Lewis. *Robert Carter of Nomini Hall.* Williamsburg: Colonial Williamsburg, Inc., 1945.

Neupert, Hanns. *The Clavichord.* Trans. Ann P. B. Feldberg. Kassel: Barenreiter-Verlag Kassel, 1965.

Nye, Russell Blaine. *The Cultural Life of the New Nation, 1776–1830.* Ed. Henry Steele Commager and Richard B. Morris. New York: Harper and Row, 1962.

O'Neal, William B. *Jefferson's Fine Arts Library for the University of Virginia.* Charlottesville, Va.: University of Virginia Press, 1956.

Peterson, Merrill D. *The Jefferson Image in the American Mind.* New York: Oxford University Press, 1960.

———. *Thomas Jefferson and the New Nation.* New York: Oxford University Press, 1970.

Roof, Katherine M. *Colonel William Smith and Lady.* Boston: Houghton Mifflin, 1929.

Russell, Raymond. *The Harpsichord and Clavichord.* London: Cassell, 1949.

Scholl, Sharon and Sylvia White. *Music and the Culture of Man.* New York: Holt, Rinehart, and Winston, 1970.

Sellers, Charles Coleman. *Charles Willson Peale.* New York: Charles Scribner's, 1969.

Shackelford, George Green, ed. *Collected Papers to Commemorate Fifty Years of the Monticello Association of the Descendants of Thomas Jefferson.* Princeton, N.J.: Princeton University Press, 1965.

Silber, Irwin, comp. and ed. *Songs America Voted By.* Harrisburg, Pa.: Stackpole Books, 1971.

Smelser, Marshall. *The Democratic Republic, 1801–1815.* Ed. Henry Steele Commager and Richard B. Morris. New York: Harper and Row, 1968.

Sonneck, Oscar G. *Early Concert Life in America (1731–1800).* Leipzig: Breitkopf und Härtel, 1907.

———. *Early Opera in America.* New York: Benjamin Blom, 1963.

———. *Francis Hopkinson and James Lyon. Two Studies in Early American Music.* 1905. Reprint. New York: Da Capo Press, 1967.

———. "*The Star Spangled Banner.*" 1914. Reprint. New York: Da Capo Press, 1969.

———. *Suum Cuique: Essays In Music.* New York: G. Schirmer, 1916.

Spaeth, Sigmund. *Read 'Em and Weep: The Songs You Forgot to Remember.* 2nd rev. ed. New York: Arco, 1945.

———. *Weep Some More, My Lady.* Garden City, N.J.: Doubleday, Page, 1927.

Spillane, Daniel. *History of the American Pianoforte, Its Technical Development, and the Trade.* 1890. Reprint. New York: Da Capo Press, 1969.

Stanard, Mary Newton. *Colonial Virginia.* Philadelphia: J. B. Lippincott, 1917.

Stevens, Denis, ed. *A History of Song.* New York: W. W. Norton, 1960.

Tallis, David. *Music Boxes: A Guide for Collectors.* New York: Stein and Day, 1971.

Tyler, Lyon G. *Letters and Times of the Tylers.* 2 vols. Richmond: Whittet and Shepperson, 1884.

Upton, William Treat. *The Art Song in America.* Boston: Oliver Ditson, 1930.

Van der Straeten, Edmund. *The History of the Violin.* 2 vols. London: Cassell, [1933].

Wharton, Anne H. *Colonial Days and Dames.* Philadelphia: J. B. Lippincott, 1895.

———. *Salons Colonial and Republican.* Philadelphia: J. B. Lippincott, 1900.

———. *Social Life in the Early Republic.* Philadelphia: J. B. Lippincott, 1902.

———. *Through Colonial Doorways.* Philadelphia: J. B. Lippincott, 1893.

Woods, Edgar. *Albemarle County in Virginia.* Bridgewater, Va.: C. J. Carrier, [1900].

Wright, Louis B. *The Cultural Life of the American Colonies, 1607–1763.* Ed. Henry Steele Commager and Richard B. Morris. New York: Harper and Row, 1962.

———. *The First Gentlemen of Virginia.* Charlottesville, Va., University Press of Virginia, 1964.

Wroth, Lawrence C. *The Colonial Printer.* 1931. Reprint. Charlottesville, Va.: University Press of Virginia, 1964.

Zuckermann, Wolfgang J. *The Modern Harpsichord: 20th Century Instruments and Their Makers.* New York: October House, 1969.

Index